Echoes of Empires

A Timeless Tapestry

By

Nathan D. Venture

Echoes of Empires

A Timeless Tapestry

Table of Contents

Introduction

Our journey through history isn't just about dates and events; it's a quest to understand the essence of human societies and what has driven them over millennia. As we venture into the astonishing saga of civilization, we aim to unravel the threads that connect our past with the present, providing a window into the forces that have shaped the world. The past holds keys to unlock timeless truths about culture, power, innovation, and resilience.

Let's ponder the vast canvas of human history. It's one that's painted with triumphs and failures, eras of peace, and chapters of turmoil. Civilizations have risen to astonishing heights, powered by colorful tapestries of culture and mind-boggling technological advancements. Yet, they've also crumbled, sometimes suddenly, leaving behind lessons etched in time. Each epoch introduces protagonists—from kings and pharaohs to inventors and revolutionaries—whose actions echo across generations.

Understanding these dynamic forces requires us to look at civilization not just as a sequence of isolated events but as an interconnected web. Throughout our exploration, we'll see how one society's innovation becomes another's foundation, sparking a ripple effect felt across continents and centuries. This vibrant exchange has birthed wonders like the pyramids in Egypt and the legal systems of ancient Rome—feats that still awe and teach us today.

This book is designed not merely as a chronology but as a mosaic of human ingenuity, adaptation, and transformation. It's about discovering how ancient farmers in Mesopotamia innovated to survive and thrive in harsh conditions, laying the groundwork for urban life. We'll see how these early advancements in agriculture sparked societal changes and how the legacy of these once great cultures persists.

Moreover, history is an epic tale of interconnectedness of power and knowledge. The rise of the Roman Empire and its subsequent fall are not just stories of conquest and collapse; they illustrate the complex balance of force and law, governance and citizenship, that has spurred modern governments globally. Similarly, the rise of China's dynasties showcases an enduring journey through periods of turmoil and glory, offering a narrative of innovation, cultural enrichment, and regeneration.

Humanity's timeline is dotted with periods of remarkable creativity and profound change—some slow and evolutional, others rapid and revolutionary. Each chapter opens a portal to these pivotal moments—be it the birth of intellectual movements or the advent of industry—all possessing ramifications that continue to reverberate through our present world. The European Enlightenment, for example, ushered in not only philosophical enlightenment but also political revolutions that redefined notions of freedom and justice.

However, history also reminds us of the stark costs of progress. The industrial revolution brought unprecedented technological leaps, yet it also triggered deep societal shifts, challenging social norms and reshaping communities. Likewise, the age of colonialism, while setting the stage for global connections, also led to long-lasting implications for societies—implications with which we are still grappling today in the narratives of decolonization and independence movements.

The chronicles of conflict, from the trenches of World War I to the ideological battlegrounds of the Cold War, reveal the dark recesses of human ambition and the relentless drive for dominance. In these tales of confrontation and struggle, we find stories not only of devastation but also of remarkable resilience and renewal, showing us how societies have rebuilt in the aftermath of war's wreckage.

As we look closer at the Information Age, we're witnessing a new kind of revolution, one of digital landscapes and instant connectivity. It's redefining borders, economies, and identities at an astonishing pace, challenging us to consider the way this era will be chronicled in the annals of time.

In closing, as we traverse these chapters, we'll draw from a wealth of visual and oral legacies, a living archive of human experience that whispers lessons from eras long passed. Within these stories of rise, fall, and rebirth, there are blueprints for future stability and innovation—reminders that the past is indeed a prologue, rich with insights for the road that stretches ahead. Let's embark on this exploration with curiosity and reflection, understanding that these stories are not just vestiges of history, but active guides in our continuous journey.

Chapter 1: Dawn of Civilization

Civilization as we know it didn't just spring up overnight. It emerged bit by bit, like a slowly unfolding drama across the vast stage of history. Human societies came together, forming communities and gradually weaving the intricate fabric of culture that would define eras. At the dawn, the world was a blank canvas, and humanity was just beginning to paint its story.

Imagine the fertile plains of ancient Mesopotamia, where early humans harnessed the mighty rivers like the Tigris and Euphrates, spurring the growth of agriculture. This was the cradle of innovation, a place where the seeds of progress were sown. The people didn't just tame the land; they began to shape their destiny with monumental leaps in technology and thought. It's astounding to think how their legacy would echo throughout time.

No one can deny the profound impact of learning to work with the land. Agriculture was more than a means of survival; it sparked the formation of cities and complex societies. With the surplus of crops, populations surged, and communities could sustain artisans, scribes, and priests, each contributing to the fabric of civilization in unique ways. Urban centers flared to life, becoming focal points of culture and innovation. Over time, these vibrant hubs sowed the seeds of what we now consider elemental to human society—laws, written language, and organized religion.

While Mesopotamia isn't the sole actor in this narrative, it undoubtedly played a starring role. Other civilizations began to emerge, each with its own distinct flair. Yet across distances and cultures, a common thread unraveled: humanity's innate drive to transform its surroundings. This unrelenting pursuit of development and understanding fueled the dawn of civilization, setting the stage for myriad achievements and challenges.

But what catalyzed this great leap toward social complexity? Part of the answer lies in the chaotic dance of necessity and invention. When faced with challenges, humans innovated. Facing harsh environments, unpredictable rivers, or even threats from rival communities, they developed new tools and strategies. The wheel, the plow, and the written word weren't just handy inventions; they were milestones in humanity's progress, each marking an advance in our civilization's capacity to thrive.

The dawn of civilization was also marked by the emergence of intricate belief systems and shared myths, which unified tribes and inspired great works of art and architecture. These shared beliefs provided cohesion and context in an unpredictable world. Temples rose from earth and stone, not only as places of worship but as testaments to human aspiration and ingenuity.

This formative period was but a prelude to the complex tapestry of human history. The foundations laid in these early societies would resonate forward, influencing civilizations across continents and epochs. As we delve deeper into the annals of history, it's clear that the dawn of civilization wasn't just a beginning—it was the start of an ever-evolving journey that continues to shape the world today.

Ancient Mesopotamia: Cradle of Innovation

In the rich tapestry of human history, Ancient Mesopotamia stands out as a beacon of early advancement. Nestled between the Tigris and

Euphrates rivers, this region, often dubbed the "Cradle of Civilization," was one of the earliest places where complex societies arose. Its people were innovators in a landscape of possibility, laying the foundational blocks of human society.

Mesopotamia is credited with creating the earliest form of writing: cuneiform. This system of writing started as simple markings on clay tablets used for record-keeping and transformed into a sophisticated means of communication. As they chronicled transactions or inscribed hymns and myths, the scribes of Mesopotamia opened the door to recorded history, allowing ideas to travel beyond oral tradition.

Beyond writing, Mesopotamians were architectural pioneers, constructing cities that reflected their growing complexity. The ziggurat, a massive terraced structure often dedicated to gods, dominated the cityscape. These monumental buildings were not just religious centers but were also expressions of the technological acumen that Mesopotamians possessed.

Two of the most enduring impacts of Mesopotamian society are their advancements in mathematics and astronomy. They developed a base-60 numerical system, a precursor to our modern timekeeping methods, dividing hours into 60 minutes and minutes into 60 seconds. Their keen observations of the stars introduced the world to a lunisolar calendar, which regulated agriculture and religious festivals.

Notably, Mesopotamia's legal structures were just as advanced as their scientific ones. The Code of Hammurabi is one of the earliest known sets of laws, illustrating a complex societal structure that was keen on maintaining order and justice. This legal framework offered insights into the everyday lives and social hierarchies of its people, providing rules that governed commerce, property, and family relations.

Agriculture was another field of innovation for the Mesopotamians. They mastered irrigation, transforming the arid landscape into fertile farmlands. This was their answer to the challenges posed by unpredictable flooding of the rivers. With surplus food came the chance for specialization in labor, fueling further advancements in various crafts and professions.

The bustling city of Ur, with its crowded streets and busy markets, served as a hub of trade and culture. Artisans flourished here, creating intricate jewelry, pottery, and textiles. These goods weren't just for local consumption; Mesopotamia's strategic location allowed it to become a pivotal player in trade networks stretching to the far reaches of the known world.

Religion played a central role in shaping Mesopotamian society. The pantheon of gods they worshipped reflected their understanding of nature and its forces. Temples were more than places of worship; they were economic powerhouses, central to city life, running workshops, storing surplus crops, and even lending resources to farmers.

Mesopotamian culture laid the foundation upon which later civilizations would build. From the structure of their governments to the ways they supplanted myths and legends with written chronicles, their innovations set the stage for future societies. As we look back at their legacy, it becomes evident that their drive to understand, shape, and improve their world is a defining trait of human civilization.

Legacy of Mesopotamian Culture

In the annals of history, Mesopotamia stands out as a beacon of early civilization, having set the stage for countless cultural advancements. Nestled between the Tigris and Euphrates rivers, this region is often referred to as the "Cradle of Civilization." It's in these fertile lands that humanity took some of its most groundbreaking steps towards organized society. From intricate city-states to the formation of some of the earliest laws, Mesopotamia's influence is both profound and enduring.

One of the most significant contributions of Mesopotamian culture is the development of writing. The Sumerians introduced cuneiform, a system of writing that would not only revolutionize communication but also lay the groundwork for record-keeping and literature. This advancement enabled them to document everything from trade transactions to epic tales, the most famous being "The Epic of Gilgamesh." Cuneiform tablets have been pivotal in understanding the social, economic, and political dynamics of ancient Mesopotamian life, painting a vivid picture of a society that thrived on knowledge and innovation.

The Mesopotamians also made extraordinary strides in law and governance, ideas that resonate to this day. The Code of Hammurabi is perhaps the most notable artifact of legal insight from this era. This set of laws was groundbreaking, not only for its detailed nature but also for its embodiment of the principle that the state had a duty to administer justice—ideas that would echo throughout history in various legal systems around the world. Hammurabi's laws were inscribed on large stone pillars, a testament to the importance of justice and order in their society.

In addition to legal frameworks, Mesopotamian innovations extended to numerous practical and scientific fields. They were pioneers in mathematics, using a base-60 system that influences how we measure time even today. This society's keen interest in astronomy led to the development of a calendar based on the moon, allowing them to predict seasons and improve agricultural productivity. The emphasis on scientific observation laid the groundwork for further advances in fields such as medicine and engineering.

Religion and mythology were deeply interwoven into the fabric of Mesopotamian culture. The pantheon of gods and goddesses, with each city-state establishing its own patron deity, reflected the complex and interconnected nature of their society. Temples and ziggurats were not just places of worship but served as community centers that facilitated economic, social, and political life. These sacred structures were architectural marvels, illustrating the Mesopotamians' ingenuity and their profound sense of spirituality.

The legacy of Mesopotamian culture is also evident in their artistry and craftsmanship. From intricate jewelry to imposing statues and detailed bas-reliefs, their art mirrored the sophisticated and diverse nature of their society. Mesopotamian artisans utilized skilled techniques that demonstrated an understanding of both aesthetics and materials, producing artifacts that continue to intrigue and inspire modern archaeologists and historians.

Mesopotamia's agricultural advancements allowed for the growth of urban centers, facilitating trade and cultural exchange. This urbanization cultivated a vibrant and dynamic society where innovation flourished. The establishment of bustling marketplaces led to the exchange of goods, ideas, and cultural practices, setting the stage for interactions among various civilizations, which fueled further advances.

Even as the empires of Mesopotamia rose and fell, their cultural ethos persisted in the empires that followed. Neighboring civilizations such as the Assyrians, Babylonians, and later, the Persians, built upon the foundation laid by Mesopotamian innovation. Each successive culture adapted and amalgamated Mesopotamian customs, ensuring the continuance of its profound influence across the ancient world.

In the grand tapestry of human history, Mesopotamia's role is undeniable. As the birthplace of many aspects of organized society, it has exerted a lasting impact on the cultures and civilizations that followed. Much of what we consider foundational to modern life can trace its lineage back to the innovations that first emerged in the land "between the rivers." The legacy of Mesopotamian culture isn't just a chapter in history books; it's the cornerstone upon which much of human progress is built.

Chapter 2: Echoes of Egypt

The Nile River was more than just a ribbon of life in the arid desert; it was Egypt's lifeline, an ongoing symphony that guided the daily rhythms of life. The floods came with predictable regularity, leaving behind fertile soil that cradled agriculture. Crops thrived, and so too did the civilization that farmed along the riverbanks. This abundance allowed the Egyptians to develop a flourishing society centered around farming, craft, and trade.

Pharaohs ruled not as mere kings, but as divine intermediaries between the gods and the people. Among them, names like Khufu and Ramesses II echo through history, amalgamating power and divinity. These rulers harnessed the resources and manpower to construct monuments that defied the odds. The pyramids of Giza, especially, stood as eternal testaments to human ingenuity and the divine order that the Egyptians believed governed their world.

Architecture reached otherworldly heights with the construction of temples dedicated to their pantheon. Painted scenes of daily life and epic battles sprawled across walls, narrating stories that transcended time. The Temple of Karnak, a sprawling complex of sanctuaries, was a testament to the religious fervor and architectural mastery of the Egyptians.

Away from the grandeur of temples and pharaohs, Egyptians also innovated in quiet yet profound ways. Their advancement in agriculture, such as the use of irrigation canals, ensured sustainable food production. This stability allowed craftspeople and scholars to pursue other fields of knowledge, from medicine to astronomy.

Ultimately, the echoes of Egypt resonated well beyond its borders. Whether it was through trade networks or cultural exchange, Egypt left its mark on subsequent civilizations. The intricate patterns of faience, medicinal recipes, and mathematical concepts traversed continents and centuries, shaping the world in subtle yet significant ways. Egypt's legacy, carved in stone and echoed in written papyrus, continues to captivate the imagination of modern observers, eager to delve deeper into this ancient civilization's secrets.

Pharaohs and the Divine Order

In the grand tapestry of ancient Egypt, the pharaohs stood as living deities, embodying both the earthly and the divine. Their presence was not just a political necessity but a cornerstone of Egyptian cosmology, bridging the human world with the ethereal realms. The pharaoh wasn't merely a king in the conventional sense but was believed to be a god among men, a successor and a son of the gods, most notably Ra, the sun god. This divine kingship established an order that was both political and spiritual, ensuring that the harmony of the universe, known as *ma'at*, was upheld.

The legitimacy of a pharaoh's reign was rooted deeply in religious doctrine. From the moment they ascended to the throne, pharaohs were entwined with the gods in a sacred partnership to maintain balance and justice in the land. The concept of *ma'at* played a crucial role in this relationship, representing truth, order, and cosmic balance. Pharaohs presented themselves as the earthly embodiments of *ma'at*, tasked with the monumental duty of protecting and perpetuating this order. Rituals, temple constructions, and offerings to the gods were not merely spiritual exercises but essential duties to ensure prosperity and stability.

It's fascinating how the royal iconography reflected the pharaohs' dual nature. They were adorned with symbols of power like the crook and flail, representing guidance and sovereignty. But more importantly, their divine stature was emphasized through the wearing of the nemes headdress and the uraeus, a symbol of divine protection. The Great Sphinx, likely bearing the likeness of Pharaoh Khafre, stands as a monumental testament to their godly visage carved in stone, meant to project their eternal vigilance over the land and its people for centuries to come.

Religious dogma wasn't the only tool pharaohs leveraged to reinforce their divine rule. Monumental architecture, such as the pyramids, stood as the ultimate assertions of their god-like status. These colossal structures served as both tombs and a testament to their eternal life, guiding souls through the afterlife and ensuring the pharaoh's continued influence in the divine realm. The construction of these edifices wasn't just about domination over nature but an articulation of cultural values, which echoed the divine order at the heart of Egyptian life. The pyramids aligned with cardinal points, mirroring celestial order and further signifying their spiritual purpose.

The influence of the pharaoh's divine mandate extended beyond their immediate reign. It penetrated the social fabric of Egypt, shaping everything from art and culture to the legal system. In a nation highly stratified by class, the divine endorsement of the pharaoh provided a sacred justification for the social hierarchy. The *viziers* and officials who served the pharaoh were seen as his direct deputies in carrying out *ma'at*. This divine endorsement transformed civil service into a sacred duty, where even the collection of taxes or the management of floodwaters was part of maintaining celestial order.

Not all pharaohs, however, adhered rigidly to this divine script. Distinct figures like Akhenaten challenged traditional religious practices by promoting a monotheistic worship of Aten, the sun disk, altering the divine landscape significantly. His rule, albeit controversial, highlighted the complexities of divine authority and the pharaoh's role in shaping religious doctrine. Despite this deviation, the subsequent restorations of polytheistic values under rulers like Tutankhamun illustrate the resilience and significance of traditional divine order in sustaining Egypt's cultural and political structure.

In the broader narrative of Egyptian history, the intertwining of divinity and kingship was integral to its prolonged legacy. This divine order didn't just reflect the religious sensibilities of the time but was a dynamic exemplar of how governance can transcend the temporal world, influencing the very cosmic order of the universe. Through the rise and fall of countless dynasties, the concept of pharaohs as living gods provided a measure of continuity and stability, a testament to the enduring power of divine kingship that was as much about governance as it was about faith.

Egyptian Innovations in Agriculture and Architecture

When we think of Egypt, it's hard not to picture the iconic pyramids rising against the desert horizon or the stately temples that echo the grandeur of ancient times. Yet, beyond these marvels of stone and geometry, ancient Egyptians made significant contributions to civilization, especially in agriculture and architecture, that resonate through time.

Far before the Greeks and Romans left their mark, Egyptians were already writing their history in mud and stone. The Nile River, with its predictable flooding, was both a boon and a challenge. Early Egyptians harnessed its cycles in ways that transformed agriculture and ensured prosperity. Their innovations in farming were not merely reactive to nature's whims; they were proactive strides that shaped a stable society.

The development of basin irrigation was among the most significant agricultural breakthroughs. This clever engineering feat allowed water retention during the flood season, ensuring crops could be grown throughout the year. Egyptians built a system of dikes, dams, and canals to manage and distribute water, which effectively sustained large populations and supported the thriving cities along the Nile. This method not only maximized the utility of the river but also spearheaded an agricultural revolution that other civilizations would later adopt.

Egyptians cultivated cereal grains like wheat and barley, staples of their diet that were pivotal in trade and sustenance. Their surplus not only fed the populace but also powered Egypt's economy, enabling wealth accumulation and supporting the development of other areas, including architecture. Storage of these grains necessitated granaries, early evidence of architectural foresight that combined utility with resilience against the elements.

The leap from mudbrick to monumental stone architecture stood as a testament to Egyptian innovation. It was a civilization with an eye to eternity, aiming to anchor its achievements in the annals of time. The pyramids, beginning with Djoser's step pyramid in Saqqara, evolved into smooth-walled constructs like the Norman pinnacle on the Giza Plateau, which likely remains the most enduring image of Egypt. Even today, the precision and scale of these structures baffle researchers and architects alike.

But why build on such a grand scale? The motivations weren't merely about grandeur or display. Architectural achievements were deeply ingrained with spiritual, political, and societal meanings. Theological beliefs about the afterlife influenced the designs and functions of these structures. Temples were more than places of worship; they were embodiments of cosmic order, bringing divine presence to earth.

The temple complexes, like those at Karnak and Luxor, were centers of worship, economic activity, and social order. They served as repositories of knowledge and art, reflecting the Egyptian worldview and cultural values. Constructed over generations, these sites reveal advances in columns and obelisks, their carvings filled with stories and triumphs, connecting the rulers to the divine.

But architectural innovation wasn't limited to the spectacular. Ordinary Egyptians lived in mudbrick houses, which, although humble, showed signs of sophisticated understanding of climate control and spatial efficiency. Houses with walls plastered and painted, sometimes with pigments that highlighted aesthetic sensibilities, provided comfort in an unforgiving desert environment. Roofs were used as functional spaces for living and storage, capitalizing on every inch of domestic architecture.

As they expanded their boundary of territory, Egyptians also advanced technologically, developing tools that improved farming and architectural endeavors. The shaduf, a manual device for lifting water, showcased the ingenuity applied to agriculture. In architecture, mathematical prowess was evident in their plans, aligning constructions with celestial phenomena, a testament to their astronomical knowledge and spiritual beliefs.

Often, we see past marvels solely through the lens of their grandeur, overshadowed by the personalities of pharaohs like Ramses or Cleopatra. Yet, the true tapestry of Egyptian achievements is woven through the everyday lives of its people, their innovations in agriculture and architecture forming the warp and weft of a civilization that thrived for millennia.

As the echoes of Egypt continue to resonate, modern individuals can observe how these ancient innovations laid foundational insights affecting qanats in Persia, providing a genesis for Roman aqueducts, and influencing irrigation methodologies across continents. Such diffusion underscores the enduring legacy of Egyptian ingenuity, diffused through time and space, inspiring continued exploration and adaptation. From Copts to modern Egyptians, the lineage of innovation remains unbroken—a perpetual homage to the fertile imaginations and unyielding spirits of their forebears who first dared to control the river, shape the stone, and dream beyond the golden horizon.

Chapter 3: The Rise and Fall of Rome

From a small settlement near the Tiber River, Rome grew into one of the most formidable empires in history. Its rise was fueled by a highly disciplined military, adept diplomacy, and a society structured to incorporate and adapt the best of the cultures it encountered. The Romans were not only conquerors; they were assimilators. They took Greek art and philosophy, Etruscan engineering, and Carthaginian trade practices, and made them their own.

The Roman Republic, initially a loose collective of territories, emerged victorious in the Punic Wars, establishing Rome as a unipolar power in the Mediterranean. Such triumphs set the stage for expansive growth. At its zenith, the Roman Empire stretched from the British Isles to the sands of Egypt, encompassing much of Europe and the Near East. This vast network allowed for the movement of people, ideas, and goods across continents, which facilitated a thriving economy and a relatively stable society for centuries.

Yet, no empire was immortal. Rome's decline was as intricate as its ascent. The seeds of downfall were planted amid the triumphs. The sheer size of the empire made it unwieldy and difficult to govern. Political corruption seeped into the fabric of Roman society, weakening the governance that had held the empire together. Economic troubles and class struggles further deepened the cracks in the Roman edifice. As external pressures mounted from barbarian tribes and internal strife grew, Rome's foundations began to crumble.

A combination of these factors led to the eventual fall of Rome in 476 AD, marking the end of the Western Roman Empire. Despite its decline, the legacy of Rome persisted, influencing Western civilization in innumerable ways. Rome's achievements in law, governance, and engineering continue to echo in modern societies, reminding us of both the heights of human capability and the potential vulnerabilities of great powers. Rome's story is a testament to the complexities and contradictions inherent in any great civilization.

Roman Military Might

Rome's military power is central to understanding how this ancient civilization rose from a small city-state to a sprawling empire. It wasn't just about swords and shields. The Romans developed a disciplined and innovative military system that allowed them to conquer vast territories over several centuries. They adapted strategies, innovated military technologies, and maintained rigorous discipline among their troops.

The Roman army's core was its legions. Each legion was composed of around 4,000 to 6,000 soldiers, primarily foot soldiers known as legionaries. These men were Roman citizens who received intense training and were expected to build not only their military skills but also their physical endurance. This training was a key factor in making the Roman army one of the most formidable forces in ancient times.

Besides their sheer numbers and training, Roman legions were well-organized. Each legion was divided into cohorts, typically consisting of 480 men, which further divided into centuries of roughly 80 soldiers each. This organization allowed for flexibility on the battlefield and made the Roman army highly adaptable to different combat situations. Commanders could deploy their forces in various formations, such as the testudo, or tortoise formation, which provided extra protection against enemy arrows.

One of the most significant innovations that contributed to Roman military success was their engineering prowess. Roman engineers could construct bridges, roads, and fortifications rapidly, enabling armies to move swiftly and securely across their empire. These infrastructures not only supported military campaigns but also facilitated the control and integration of conquered territories.

Roman military tactics were also influential. They adopted and modified techniques from their enemies. For example, after early defeats by the Celtiberians, they incorporated some of their strategies. The Romans weren't above hiring foreign mercenaries when they needed specialized skills that their own troops didn't possess. This openness to different military traditions and technologies kept the Roman army adaptable and modern for much of its existence.

Discipline was another cornerstone of Roman military might. Soldiers were expected to adhere to strict codes of conduct, and deviation from these often met with severe punishment. This rigor ensured that Roman soldiers were reliable and obedient, traits that significantly contributed to their battlefield successes. Moreover, promotions within the ranks were based on merit rather than birthright or political connections, leading to a motivated and capable leadership.

Yet, the military was more than just a tool for conquest. It was also a means of Romanization, spreading Roman culture, language, and laws throughout the empire. As soldiers settled in conquered regions after their service, they blended local traditions with Roman customs. This cultural integration created a more cohesive empire.

Technology played a key role in maintaining Roman military dominance. The Romans developed advanced weaponry and armor, such as the gladius, a short sword perfect for close-quarters combat, and the pilum, a heavy javelin designed to penetrate enemy shields.

Their siege engines, like the ballista and onager, allowed them to lay waste to enemy fortifications with terrifying efficiency.

As the Roman Empire expanded, maintaining such a vast territory required not only military might but also strategic alliances. The Romans were adept diplomats, often aligning with local leaders to maintain peace in newly-conquered regions. This combination of military strength and strategic alliances allowed Rome to hold onto its dominion for centuries.

However, this expansion had its drawbacks. The further the empire stretched, the more difficult it became to manage. Communication times lagged, and local revolts became more frequent. The once-reliable Roman legions began to rely more heavily on non-Roman recruits, who didn't always have the same loyalty to Rome. These cracks in the mighty Roman military system became precursors to the eventual decline of the empire.

In reflecting on the rise and fall of Rome, it becomes clear that its military might was both a strength and a vulnerability. While it secured Rome's place as a dominant force, the overreliance on military solutions to political and economic problems eventually contributed to its decline. This complex interplay serves as a testament to how power and discipline can elevate an empire and also foreshadows the need for adaptability and foresight in the stewardship of that power.

Legacy of Roman Law and Governance

The Roman Empire, with its unmatched expanse and influence, left behind a legacy that reverberates through the corridors of history. And while its military prowess is often credited for its rise to dominance, it was Rome's formidable system of law and governance that laid the foundation for its enduring influence. The Roman legal framework, both innovative and comprehensive, served as a vital instrument in unifying the sprawling territories under its control.

At the heart of Roman law was the principle of *ius civile*, the civil law that applied to Roman citizens. Over time, as Rome expanded, the necessity for a more inclusive system led to the development of the *ius gentium*, or the law of nations, applicable to foreigners and their interactions with citizens. This adaptation was a pragmatic stroke, crucial in managing a diverse empire of multiple cultures and communities. Rome's legal architecture didn't just dictate policies; it became a cultural lingua franca that spoke to citizens and non-citizens alike, easing tensions and forging a collective identity.

The Twelve Tables, often considered the cornerstone of Roman law, marked a significant leap towards a system based on transparency and equality. Established around 450 BCE, these laws weren't just carved onto silver; they were etched into the heart of Roman culture, laying out fundamental rights and procedures that would inform later legal traditions. Concepts of property, inheritance, and personal rights were outlined, forming the backbone of Roman civil society. The clarity and accessibility of these laws were revolutionary, setting precedents that other civilizations would emulate.

Despite its ancient origins, the influence of Roman law is palpable even today. The notion of equity, the promotion of public law over personal vendettas, and the idea that laws should be written and publicly accessible, owe much to Roman innovations. The medieval revival of Roman law, particularly in Western Europe, laid the framework for modern legal systems. Canon law and civil law systems seen in many parts of the world have their roots intricately tied to Roman legal principles, demonstrating the timelessness of its judicial strategies.

But it wasn't just the content of Roman law that left its mark; it was also about its administration. The Roman Republic, and later the Imperial system, showcased a structure where various assemblies, magistrates, and the Senate played vital roles in governance. This balanced division of powers, though not always devoid of corruption or conflict, demonstrated a keen understanding of human governance. The checks and balances of power in Roman political systems echo in contemporary governmental structures, particularly that of republicanism and democracy.

The role of a strong, centralized administration was another pillar of Roman governance. The establishment of bureaucratic institutions, capable of tax collection, infrastructure maintenance, and military organization, showcased Rome's capability to govern effectively over vast distances. These institutions were vital in maintaining order and prosperity, proving that Rome understood the importance of governance beyond mere conquest. Provinces, ruled by governors appointed by Rome, had to balance local customs with imperial mandates, a delicate act that required deft political maneuvering.

Furthermore, the importance Rome placed on public participation was forward-thinking. Although not perfect by any means—since full participation was restricted to free male citizens—it laid the groundwork for ideas of citizenship and civic duty. Political participation, through voting and public discourse, fostered a population deeply involved in their state's functioning, hints of which are seen in the citizen representations we value today.

Over centuries, as internal strife and external pressures began to unravel the Roman Empire, its legal and governmental legacy persisted. The codification efforts of Justinian I, known as the Corpus Juris Civilis, were a monumental effort to systematize Roman law in the 6th century. This compilation was instrumental in preserving Roman legal thought, serving as a cornerstone for legal education and practice in the Byzantine Empire and later in Western Europe, where it influenced the development of the legal profession.

Moreover, Roman governance left its imprint on urban planning and administrative rationality. Roman cities weren't just centers of power; they were meticulously planned entities with forums, basilicas, and amphitheaters that embodied Roman organizational genius. Roads, aqueducts, and bridges, built with immense skill and foresight, facilitated commerce and communication across the empire. This commitment to infrastructure not only bolstered trade and economic stability but also symbolized the connectivity and unity that Rome aspired to maintain across its territories.

The legacy of Roman law and governance is more than just remnants of a bygone empire; it is a testament to Rome's capacity to blend pragmatism with innovation in crafting systems that addressed the complex realities of ruling diverse populations. Its principles of legal clarity, the notion of a unified law over factional justice, and systemic governance resonate with contemporary societies striving for equity and order. As we navigate our intricate world, Rome's legacy offers both lessons and inspiration, reminding us of the potential for human ingenuity and governance to shape the evolution of civilization itself.

Chapter 4:
China's Dynastic Tapestry

The vast history of China is a story that unfolds through its dynasties, each dynasty adding a new layer to its complex tapestry. These ruling families not only altered the political landscape but also redefined the cultural and social fabric of the country. The concept of the "Mandate of Heaven" played a crucial role in this dynastic cycle, legitimizing rulers and justifying the rise and fall of kingdoms. Leaders needed to earn the favor of both the divine and the people, a delicate balance that governed the transitions between dynasties.

China's ancient beginnings were marked by the consolidation of power under the legendary Xia, Shang, and Zhou dynasties, setting the stage for more familiar names that followed. Each dynasty contributed its own innovations and philosophies, which have left a lasting impact on Chinese culture and governance. The Qin Dynasty, though short-lived, achieved remarkable feats, including the construction of the Great Wall and the unification of China's warring states under a centralized bureaucracy.

Unlike its predecessors, the Han Dynasty heralded a golden age of economic prosperity, cultural flourishing, and territorial expansion, which solidified China's place as a leading civilization of its time. Confucian ideals were institutionalized, shaping the ethical and moral compass of the society and government. Silk Road trade routes blossomed, connecting China with far-off lands and facilitating the exchange of goods, ideas, and technology.

The story is not without turmoil. Dynasties like the Ming and Qing waxed and waned under the pressure of internal strife and external threats. The inevitable decline of these dynasties opened the door to modern China, with its revolutionary changes that sought to redefine what it means to be Chinese in a rapidly evolving world.

Each transition was a canvas where new strokes were painted, leaving traces that modern scholars continue to piece together today. China's dynastic history is not merely a reminiscing of past events but a foundation for understanding the nation's current identity and aspirations.

Han Dynasty: Golden Age of China

The Han Dynasty, an era that spanned four centuries from 206 BCE to 220 CE, casts a long shadow over Chinese history. It was a period marked by remarkable prosperity, cultural richness, and territorial expansion, often heralded as China's Golden Age. How did this dynasty assemble such a formidable legacy, and what threads of the past did it weave into the fabric of Chinese civilization? Understanding these questions requires a dive into the key attributes that made the Han Dynasty unique and influential.

Emerging from the turmoil of the Qin Dynasty's fall, the Han Dynasty took root under the leadership of Liu Bang, later known as Emperor Gaozu. Unlike the oppressive policies of their predecessors, the Han emperors recognized the importance of balancing strict legalism with the Confucian ideals of governance. They believed in an administration led by merit rather than birthright, which was somewhat revolutionary for its time. This philosophy allowed for a more stable and efficient bureaucracy that facilitated the Han's long-lasting reign.

Perhaps what makes the Han Dynasty truly standout is its commitment to Confucianism. While previous dynasties had given

Confucian ideas a nod, it was the Han who institutionalized them. Confucian teachings became the bedrock of education and public ethics, shaping not just political decisions but societal behavior, too. The civil service examination, which drew heavily on Confucian classics, became a tool for selecting officials—a practice that resonated through future dynasties and beyond.

Beyond governance, the Han period was a crucible for cultural and technological advancements. It was during this time that paper—a simple yet transformative invention—was developed. Paper would revolutionize the way people recorded history, communicated, and disseminated knowledge. Moreover, the Han era witnessed strides in astronomy, medicine, and engineering, paving the way for innovations like the seismograph and advancements in silk production, which was already a highly prized commodity in both local and international trade circuits.

The Silk Road, the legendary trade route that connected China with the West, blossomed under the Han Dynasty. It wasn't just goods that traveled this route; ideas, religion, and culture flowed freely along these ancient paths. This network not only enriched the Chinese economy but also facilitated cultural exchanges. Buddhism, for instance, found its way into China through these routes, providing an alternative spiritual framework to the traditional Confucian and Taoist beliefs.

On the military front, the Han Dynasty wasn't one to rest on its laurels. It pushed the frontiers of the Chinese Empire, extending its reach deep into Central Asia, Korea, and Vietnam. These new territories weren't just about conquest; they were essential for controlling the Silk Road trade routes. With these expansions, the Han managed not just to gain access to valuable resources but also to bring diverse groups into the empire's fold, thus enriching its cultural tapestry.

Socially, the Han era was marked by a hierarchy that, while rigid, provided a sense of order and stability. The family remained the central unit of society; patriarchal structures were reinforced, but it also laid down the framework for a society where social mobility was possible through education and service. Marriage and kinship ties were avenues to strengthen political alliances and consolidate power.

The Han Dynasty faced its share of challenges as well. Natural disasters, corrupt officials, and occasional uprisings put pressure on the imperial administration. However, the Han's ability to adapt—whether by reforming policies, embracing new ideas, or modifying its system of governance—allowed it to maintain control and achieve longevity that was unmatched by subsequent short-lived dynasties.

The Han Empire's eventual downfall came from internal strife and external pressures. The latter part of the dynasty saw a weakened central control due to competing factions at court, eunuch interference in politics, and peasant rebellions such as the one led by the Yellow Turbans. As economic hardships mounted and natural calamities took their toll, the cohesion that had once defined the Han infrastructure began to unravel. Yet even in its decline, the dynasty laid the groundwork for future Chinese unity and identity.

In retrospect, the Han Dynasty's impacts are profoundly enduring. It set standards in governance and culture that continued to influence China until the modern era. If you peer into Chinese culture today, you will find that echoes of the Han period are still evident, whether in phrases, customs, or the very language itself, as the written script evolved significantly during this time.

To fully appreciate the Han Dynasty's legacy is to acknowledge the foundational role it played not just in Chinese history but in world history too. It was a time when China defined what it meant to be a thriving society, a beacon of governance, culture, and innovation that other civilizations looked to and learned from. Thus, the Han Dynasty remains a cornerstone in the study of China's dynastic past, serving as a point of reference when examining the ebbs and flows of its vast historical narrative.

Fall of the Qing and the Rise of Modern China

The collapse of the Qing Dynasty marked a turning point in China's history, shaping the foundation of the modern nation we know today. This era, charged with turmoil and transformation, unraveled the old imperial order and set the stage for revolutionary changes. For over two centuries, the Qing had ruled China's vast territories, but by the mid-19th century, increasing internal strife and foreign pressures weakened their grip.

To understand the Qing Dynasty's fall, one must look at the internal challenges they faced. The Taiping Rebellion, which began in 1850, was one of the most devastating civil conflicts in history, costing millions of lives over a 14-year span. The Taiping leaders capitalized on widespread dissatisfaction with the Qing government, which was perceived as corrupt and ineffective. This rebellion exposed the vulnerabilities of a dynasty struggling to maintain control over its diverse populace.

While the Qing battled internal dissension, external pressures mounted. Foreign powers, notably Britain and France, forced China into a series of "unequal treaties," eroding Chinese sovereignty and economic stability. The Opium Wars, instigated by the British to protect their lucrative trade in opium, exposed China's military frailties. The Treaty of Nanking, signed in 1842, ceded Hong Kong to Britain and granted foreign nationals privileges that undermined Qing authority.

In addition to mounting military and political challenges, economic strains amplified the dynasty's troubles. China, once self-sufficient, found itself at the mercy of foreign influence in major coastal trading cities. The influx of foreign goods destabilized traditional industries and deepened poverty among rural populations. Within these economic chasms, seeds of dissent were sown, nurturing revolutionary ideals among intellectuals and reformists eager for change.

By the late 19th century, China's intellectual climate shifted dramatically. A growing number of scholars called for reform, questioning both Qing rule and traditional Chinese society. Inspired by global ideas and revolutions, such as the successful Meiji Restoration in Japan, Chinese reformers sought to modernize education, governance, and technology. Efforts like the Self-Strengthening Movement aimed to blend modern innovations with traditional Chinese values, though many reform attempts fizzled due to bureaucratic resistance.

Amid this backdrop of unrest and reform, a significant figure emerged: Sun Yat-sen. Often hailed as the father of modern China, Sun advocated for a republic, a concept that resonated with many frustrated by the Qing's failures. His vision for a new China was pinned on three core principles: nationalism, democracy, and livelihood. Sun's role in the 1911 revolution was instrumental, sparking the events that would eventually dismantle imperial rule.

The 1911 Revolution, also known as the Xinhai Revolution, effectively ended over two thousand years of imperial rule in China. Key uprisings in cities like Wuhan ignited nationwide support, and by early 1912, the Qing Dynasty officially abdicated. This transition, though jubilant for many, was fraught with challenges as China grappled with establishing a unified republic from the remnants of an empire.

With the Qing's abdication, the Republic of China was born, but unity was elusive. Warlord factions vied for control in the political vacuum, and regional allegiances often took precedence over national identity. The fledgling government faced immense pressure to deliver the promises of revolution while staving off external threats and managing internal discord.

Yet, amid these turbulent times, modernization efforts gained traction. Educational reform flourished, new universities opened, and students flocked to study overseas, bringing back novel ideas and a thirst for progress. Industrialization, though uneven, began to sprout, especially in urban centers where burgeoning railways and factories symbolized a break from the past.

The rise of modern China was not a straight path but a complex journey influenced by both internal ambitions and external influences. Sun Yat-sen's vision found varying degrees of success and set the ideological bedrock for future leaders. Mao Zedong and the founding of the People's Republic of China in 1949 can trace their roots to the revolutionary ideas that burgeoned during this critical transition period.

As one reflects on the fall of the Qing Dynasty and the rise of modern China, it's evident that this transformation was not merely a political shift but a deep societal evolution. The legacy of this era echoes in China's contemporary quest for global stature, embodying a nation's resilience and adaptability in the face of immense change.

Today's China, with its rapid technological advancement and economic prowess, bears the indelible marks of its dynastic past and revolutionary transitions. At its core lies a story of perseverance and redefinition, propelled by those who dared to dream of a new dawn for their country amid the twilight of the Qing emperors.

Chapter 5: The Medieval Matrix

The medieval world was a complex web of interactions and power dynamics, sometimes appearing chaotic yet following a distinct structure: the feudal system. This era, often referred to as the Middle Ages, spanned roughly from the 5th to the late 15th century. It was a time where the decline of Roman centralized control allowed for the rise of localized power held by lords in Europe. These lords governed their land with the help of vassals who pledged loyalty and military support in exchange for protection and the right to work sections of the land.

Feudal society operated like a massive network, each connection crucial to its overall stability. Lords managed not just land, but law and justice within their territories, acting as mini-sovereigns. Peasants worked the land, paying taxes and laboring for the lords, who in turn offered protection against external threats and internal squabbles. The idea wasn't just economics; it was about mutual obligations and loyalty that glued communities together, despite the apparent inequalities.

Amid this structured chaos, the role of the church became monumental. The medieval church wasn't just a spiritual institution; it wielded political power, influencing kings and shaping policies across Europe. Religious leaders often had the ear of monarchs, guiding decisions in matters of state. The church's reach into education and knowledge meant that it was a pivotal custodian of ideas, preserving ancient texts and fostering scholastic endeavors. Monasteries became centers of learning and literacy, offering a glimmer of enlightenment during turbulent times.

However, the matrix of medieval society was not static. Toward the later Middle Ages, significant societal shifts began to take shape. The growing power of cities, spurred by commerce and trade, started to challenge the traditional feudal hierarchy. Guilds emerged, representing collective interests of craftsmen and merchants, gradually strengthening urban influence over rural dominion. This rise of commerce not only transformed economies but also catalyzed social shifts, making societal structures more fluid.

The concept of chivalry, an idealized code of conduct for knights, added another layer to the social fabric, emphasizing honor, bravery, and courtesy. Although often romanticized today, the chivalric code sought to bind warriors to a higher standard of behavior in both war and peace. These ideals helped justify and fuel the numerous conflicts which stained medieval landscapes, from the Crusades to internal feudal skirmishes.

As powerful as the medieval matrix was in maintaining order, it was not immune to challenges. Famines, plagues, and wars began to tear at its seams, as societies struggled to adapt to changing conditions. Feudal obligations sometimes strained under the weight of unavoidable catastrophes. The Black Death, for instance, decimated populations, prompting shifts in labor dynamics and weakening feudal bonds.

In examining the medieval matrix, we glimpse a world that struggled to balance its structures and demands against the need for growth and adaptability. The interplay of rigid hierarchy and emergent flexibility laid the groundwork for the development of modern states, establishing patterns which continue to echo through the corridors of history. This connection to the past informs our understanding of societal architecture, offering insights into the dynamics of human civilization today.

Feudal Europe: Lords and Vassals

In the fabric of medieval Europe, the system of feudalism emerged as a complex web of obligations and allegiances, deeply interwoven with the daily lives of individuals from every social strata. It wasn't just a political system; it was a social and economic structure that dictated the dynamics of power and land ownership. Feudalism shaped the European landscape, creating a hierarchy that was both rigid and fluid, depending on one's perspective.

Central to this system were the lords and vassals, whose relationships were rooted in mutual benefit and loyalty. At the heart of the feudal arrangement was the fief—a parcel of land granted by a lord to a vassal in exchange for military service and various obligations. This exchange was formalized through a ceremony known as "homage and fealty," where the vassal pledged allegiance to the lord, kneeling and placing his hands between those of the lord. It was a solemn affair, binding both parties to their commitments.

Lords, possessing vast tracts of land, wielded significant authority and influence. They were the king's vassals, yet in their own domains, they exercised near-kingly power. A lord's primary role was to provide protection to his vassals and manage the lands under his control. This management often involved adjudicating disputes among vassals, overseeing agricultural production, and ensuring the defense of the territory.

In contrast, the vassals had a different set of responsibilities. Although they were granted land, this gift wasn't free from obligations. Vassals were expected to provide military service, a duty that could include everything from serving in the lord's army to assisting in castle defense. They might also be required to attend the lord's court, offer counsel, or provide financial aid, particularly through aid payments for special events, such as the knighting of the lord's son or the marriage of his daughter.

It's important to recognize that the feudal system was not uniform across Europe. While the basic tenets of feudalism were similar, regional variations existed that affected how these relationships played out in practice. In some areas, the ties between lords and vassals were more informal, while in others, they were stringently adhered to.

The system was heavily reliant on personal relationships and mutual respect. The social contract inherent in feudal ties was reinforced by kinship ties, marriage alliances, and even social events. Lords and vassals often shared familial bonds, complicating the web of alliances and obligations. Such bonds could bring stability but also sow the seeds of conflict, as personal grievances sometimes played themselves out on a larger political stage.

At times, this network of loyalties and obligations led to conflicts, particularly when loyalties were divided or when lords demanded more than their vassals could or were willing to provide. Vassals could find themselves caught between conflicting loyalties if they held fiefs from more than one lord. Feudalism, for all its stability, was prone to these internal conflicts, which could escalate into larger wars among competing factions.

Interestingly, the power dynamics within the feudal system were not entirely one-sided. While lords held significant power, vassals, too, wielded influence, particularly collectively. A strong and unified group of vassals could exert pressure on a lord, restraining an oppressive or overly ambitious ruler. This balance of power was less visible but crucial to the stability of the feudal hierarchy.

The Church also played a pivotal role in the feudal order. Monasteries and bishoprics were major landholders, and church leaders were often lords in their own right. The Church influenced feudal relationships through its moral authority and its ability to legitimize rulers. It also provided a counterbalance to secular power, sometimes mediating conflicts between lords and vassals.

Over the centuries, the nature of these feudal bonds evolved. As European societies expanded and economies grew more complex, some aspects of feudalism became less rigid. The rise of trade, urban centers, and monetary economies began to undermine the land-based power of the traditional lords. By the late Middle Ages, the system started to transform, setting the stage for the modern nation-states that would emerge.

Nonetheless, the legacy of feudal lords and vassals remains deeply embedded in European culture and history. This medieval matrix, with its intricate tapestry of relationships, laid down a foundation that influenced social and political structures far beyond its original time and place.

Societal Shifts in the Later Middle Ages

The Later Middle Ages, roughly from the 11th to the 15th centuries, was a period packed with transformation and transition. As we delve into the complex changes of this era, it's crucial to understand the backdrop of a society teetering on the brink of modernity while still tethered to its feudal roots. This was a time when the rigid structures of feudalism began to give way to more dynamic social and economic configurations.

One of the most significant shifts occurred in the realm of economic life. The later Middle Ages saw the gradual decline of manorialism, the economic system that had dominated rural Europe for centuries. A combination of factors, including the Black Death, led to a sharp decrease in the population, which in turn resulted in labor shortages. Suddenly, serfs and peasants found themselves in a position to demand better wages and improved working conditions. This new economic reality upset the traditional feudal order and laid the groundwork for the rise of a more market-oriented economy.

The depopulation sparked by the Black Death also bolstered urbanization. As agricultural productivity increased, more people migrated to cities in search of opportunities. These burgeoning urban centers became hotspots of commerce and trade, leading to the growth of a burgeoning middle class. Artisans, merchants, and craftsmen began to establish themselves as an influential force in society, challenging the longstanding dominance of the aristocracy.

Yet, economic changes weren't the only transformations taking place. There was a discernible shift in intellectual life as well. The later Middle Ages witnessed a revival in scholarly activity that would eventually culminate in the Renaissance. This period, often termed the "12th-century Renaissance," saw the reintroduction of ancient Greek and Roman texts via translations from Arabic scholars. Universities began to spring up across Europe, providing venues for intellectual exchange and debate. The emphasis on reason and inquiry started to reshape medieval thought, setting the stage for future advancements.

Against this backdrop of intellectual renewal, another critical societal shift was the rising tension between religious and secular authorities. The power dynamic between church and state was in flux, with monarchies consolidating power and asserting independence from ecclesiastical influence. This shift reached its zenith with events like the Avignon Papacy and the Great Schism, which exposed the vulnerabilities and corruption within the Church and sowed seeds of dissatisfaction among the populace. The weakening of papal authority was a precursor to the Reformation movements that would follow in later centuries.

Technological advancements were also at play during this time. The invention of the heavy plow and three-field system revolutionized agriculture, improving efficiency and crop yields. These innovations, coupled with developments in wind and water mill technology, transformed rural economies and indirectly supported population growth and urban expansion. Moreover, the introduction of inventions like the compass and astrolabe spurred exploration and trade across new maritime routes, widening Europe's horizons and economic sphere.

Socially, the later Middle Ages saw a gradual shift in gender roles and family structures. The legal and economic reforms during this time opened doors for women to be more actively involved in trade and commerce. While the patriarchal norms remained dominant, the post-Black Death era sometimes necessitated women's involvement in managing estates and businesses due to the loss of male family members. This evolution marked a slow but significant change in societal attitudes towards gender roles.

Political structures also experienced notable shifts as kingdoms and nation-states began to coalesce into more centralized entities. The feudal bonds of loyalty and obligation that tied vassals to lords started to fray as monarchs exercised more direct control over their territories. The introduction of new taxation systems and standing armies reduced the nobility's power and curtailed their influence over regional governance. England's Magna Carta and France's Estates-General are exemplars of evolving governance that sought balance between sovereign power and subjects' rights.

While the Later Middle Ages presented numerous challenges, including famines, plagues, and wars, it was a period rich with societal evolution. The economic, intellectual, and political transformations collectively propelled Europe toward a more modern framework, inadvertently setting the stage for the dynamic upheavals of the Renaissance and the Enlightenment. This transitional era was both a conclusion and a beginning—a close to the medieval worldview and an advent of societal modernity.

Chapter 6: Enlightenment and Revolution

The Enlightenment was an era that sparked immense intellectual awakening. From the dimly lit rooms of Parisian salons to the bustling streets of London, a wave of new ideas challenged the status quo. Thinkers like Voltaire, Locke, and Rousseau questioned the very foundations of society, advocating for reason, freedom, and a more just social order. Their writings created ripples that extended well beyond European borders, challenging traditional authorities and igniting debates on governance, rights, and human potential.

During this period, the notion of individual rights began to gain ground. Philosophers argued that every person was entitled to life, liberty, and property. Monarchies and the divine right of kings faced scrutiny and skepticism as people started envisioning societies governed by the will of the people rather than inherited power. It wasn't just talk; these ideas began to be reflected in political reform across continents. Words on paper turned into reforms and revolutions, setting the stage for profound change.

The American Revolution proved to be a turning point, embodying Enlightenment ideals in action. Fueled by a desire for self-governance and freedom from tyrannical rule, the colonists embarked on a journey toward nationhood. They drafted the Declaration of Independence in 1776, a document steeped in the spirit of Enlightenment thought. The struggle for American independence was not just a local conflict but rather a beacon of inspiration, encouraging similar movements across the globe. The revolution demonstrated the tangible power of Enlightenment thinking, showing that societies could indeed reshape themselves in pursuit of liberty and equality.

This era laid the groundwork for modern democracies and still echoes in contemporary political philosophy. It was a time where thinkers dared to dream of a better world, and societies began to transform those dreams into reality. In an age that questioned everything, the sparks of Enlightenment lit the way for revolutions, forever altering the trajectory of human history.

Intellectual Currents of the Enlightenment

The Enlightenment wasn't just a period; it was a lively exchange of ideas that set the stage for modern thinking. It sparked a significant transformation in how people viewed the world and their place in it. This intellectual upheaval questioned traditional authority and embraced the power of human reason. It greatly influenced the society, politics, and economies of the time, laying down a blueprint for modern democratic and scientific institutions.

At the heart of the Enlightenment was a profound shift in how knowledge was pursued and understood. Scholars, known as philosophes, sought to apply reason and scientific method to all aspects of life. This rational approach challenged the dogmas of the Church and monarchical authority, ultimately arguing that individuals should rely more on their own intellect than on inherited wisdom. Notable minds like Voltaire, John Locke, and Immanuel Kant were torchbearers in this new way of thinking. Each articulated visions of freedom, individual rights, and equality that would ripple through the centuries.

This era encouraged the flourishing of the public sphere—a realm where individuals could debate and exchange ideas openly. Coffee houses, salons, and literary circles became pivotal centers for discussion, allowing ideas to mingle and evolve. These venues were not just physical spaces but emblematic of a new culture of dialogue. The philosophies discussed in these places would soon transcend social boundaries and ignite movements toward political and social reforms.

Locke's theories on government and human nature were particularly groundbreaking. He imagined a society where governance was rooted in the consent of the governed, a radical idea that stood starkly against the entrenched notions of divine-right monarchy. He argued for a social contract where the rulers' authority rested on an agreement with the people, who retained the ultimate power to overthrow a failing ruler. Locke's ideas on life, liberty, and property laid critical groundwork for modern political thought and heavily influenced revolutionary movements in the Americas and beyond.

Voltaire, with his wit and incisive criticism, took up arms against authority and intolerance, championing freedom of speech and religious tolerance. His biting criticisms of established institutions and advocacy for civil liberties were instrumental in the debate over the separation of church and state. While Voltaire primarily targeted the tyranny of the French monarchy and the Church, his ideas resonated across borders, fanning the flames of resistance and reform.

The Enlightenment's intellectual currents also carried scientific inquiry to new horizons. Figures like Isaac Newton and René Descartes were pivotal in this scientific revolution, emphasizing empirical evidence and mathematical logic over speculation. Newton's laws of motion and universal gravitation illustrated the power of reason and observation, influencing not only scientific fields but also the philosophical outlooks of the age. This new scientific mindset fostered a shift from superstition to a trust in the power of human reason and the potential for progress.

The era's emphasis on reason and individualism somewhat sidetracked religious dogma yet didn't entirely dismiss spirituality.

Enlightenment thinkers like Rousseau sought a balance, advocating for a "natural religion" that was more aligned with personal ethics and emotional engagement than institutional rites. This marked a significant departure from the rigid orthodoxy of previous centuries, integrating an appreciation for nature and emotion with the era's rational pursuits.

While the Enlightenment was largely a Western phenomenon, its intellectual currents reached far beyond Europe. The colonial powers spread Enlightenment ideas to their colonies, influencing nascent independence movements and spurring debates on human rights and governance around the world. The impact of Enlightenment thought didn't just stop with political borders; it permeated cultures and fueled ambitions for self-determination and democratic representation worldwide.

This transformative period set the stage for future revolutions, notably the American and French revolutions, which translated Enlightenment philosophies into tangible political action. Ideas of liberty, equality, and fraternity endured as central themes, echoing through the centuries in various democratic transformations and human rights campaigns across the globe.

Ultimately, the Enlightenment was a crucible of thought, melding varying streams of philosophy, science, and innovation into a movement that shaped the modern world. It urged societies to abandon the confines of tradition, to question rather than accept, and to seek knowledge through reason. In this way, the Enlightenment's intellectual currents were not merely academic debates of a bygone era but live wires that continue to ignite discussions about freedom, progress, and humanity's capacity for change.

American Revolution: A New Dawn

The American Revolution marked a pivotal era, not just for North America, but for the world. It was a time when ideas of liberty, self-governance, and equality began to solidify. The movement toward independence didn't spring up overnight. It simmered over decades, a response to the growing strain between the American colonies and the British crown.

In the years leading up to the revolution, Britain's seemingly endless string of taxes and laws felt like a noose tightening around colonial necks. The Stamp Act of 1765, the Townshend Acts of 1767, and the notorious Tea Act of 1773 were just a few examples of the burdens placed on the colonists. Each act seemed to provoke more outrage than the last, fueling a collective desire for autonomy.

But it wasn't just taxes that riled the colonists. The philosophical undercurrents at play were equally powerful. Enlightenment thinkers like John Locke and Jean-Jacques Rousseau had planted seeds that would grow into a fierce yearning for self-determination. Concepts like natural rights, the social contract, and the sovereignty of the people began to resonate deeply with many colonists, turning abstract philosophy into actionable ideas.

The famous slogan "No taxation without representation" became a rallying cry. It wasn't just about taxes—it was about power and who held it. The people wanted their voices heard, their opinions counted. For them, true justice meant having a say in the laws that affected their daily lives.

The spark that would ignite the revolution was undoubtedly the confrontations at Lexington and Concord in April 1775. When the first shots were fired, the colonies were drawn into a full-blown conflict with Britain. Though it began as a fight for rights as British subjects, it rapidly evolved into a struggle for complete independence.

The Declaration of Independence, penned by Thomas Jefferson in 1776, was a bold statement to the world. It laid out the colonies' grievances against the British crown but also outlined an optimistic vision of a new, independent nation. The document's influence stretched far beyond the immediate demands of its signatories; it inspired future generations seeking freedom and justice.

Throughout the war, the American forces were often outmanned, outgunned, and outmaneuvered by the professional British military. What they lacked in resources, though, they made up with tenacity and a growing network of support from abroad. France's entry into the war in 1778 proved invaluable, providing the critical military aid that helped turn the tide in favor of the Americans.

The Treaty of Paris in 1783 formally ended the war, with Britain recognizing the independence of the United States. It was a monumental victory, but it was also the beginning of another complex journey: forming a new nation. With independence won, the daunting task of constructing a functional, stable democracy lay ahead.

The drafting of the United States Constitution in 1787 was a groundbreaking moment. Debates raged over how power should be distributed, how much authority the federal government should wield compared to states, and how to balance the often-competing interests of different regions and social classes. The resulting document was a blend of innovative governance principles and pragmatic compromises.

Throughout this transformative era, individuals played critical roles. Figures like George Washington emerged as symbols of unity and integrity. Washington's leadership was instrumental both during the war and in the early years of the new republic. His decision to step down after two terms as president set an essential precedent for democratic transition.

The revolution was as much a cultural and social phenomenon as it was a political and military one. It inspired movements worldwide, sparking ideas of republicanism in places as far-flung as France and Latin America. The idea that people could overthrow long-standing systems of monarchy and colonial rule resonated far beyond American shores.

Yet, the revolution's promises were not universal. Slavery remained a glaring contradiction to the ideals espoused in the Declaration, and the rights of women and Native Americans were largely ignored in the new framework of governance. These shortcomings marked significant challenges that the young nation would grapple with for generations.

Despite these challenges, the American Revolution remains a defining moment in history. It defied conventional wisdom by proving that a determined populace could defeat one of the world's most powerful empires. More than that, it set a new standard for what a society could aspire to—a society built on principles of freedom, equality, and democracy.

As history continued to unfold, the revolution's legacy evolved. The triumphs and challenges it presented continue to be topics of reflection and debate. Through it all, the founding ideals have served as both inspiration and caution, compelling us to confront the complexities of liberty and governance as we forge the future.

Chapter 7: Industrial Revolution: Forging a New World

The Industrial Revolution marked a profound transformation that reshaped societies and economies at an unprecedented pace. Emerging in the late 18th century, it fundamentally altered the way humans lived and worked. It wasn't just a shift from agrarian economies to industrial powerhouses; it was the dawn of a new era characterized by innovation and change. Steam engines, textile machines, and ironworks became the symbols of this radical overhaul.

At the heart of it all was the incredible proliferation of new technologies. Factories sprung up, teeming with workers who operated machines that produced goods faster and more efficiently than ever before. James Watt's improvements on the steam engine powered machinery that replaced manpower on a massive scale. Richard Arkwright's spinning frame and Edmund Cartwright's power loom revolutionized the textile industry, turning Great Britain into the world's workshop.

As technology advanced, so did the demands on society. Populations grew as people flocked to cities in search of work. This urban migration led to the development of massive metropolitan areas. Cities like Manchester and Birmingham swelled in size almost overnight, creating both opportunities and challenges. Urban life came with a litany of social issues—overcrowded tenements, unsanitary conditions, and the rise of a working class that toiled long hours under often harsh conditions.

But the impacts of the Industrial Revolution weren't contained to just technological advances and urban growth. It altered the social fabric of societies. Traditional family roles shifted as both men and women sought employment in factories. Child labor became a contentious issue, prompting debates about workers' rights and paving the way for future reformations. The working-class movement began to gain momentum, questioning the fairness of wealth distribution brought about by such rapid industrialization.

The ripple effects spread beyond borders. Europe saw a wave of industrial fervor that soon reached America. By the mid-19th century, the United States was forging ahead, adopting and expanding upon British technologies. This transatlantic exchange of ideas and innovations fueled further growth and led to monumental infrastructural projects like railways and canals that connected distant regions, facilitating commerce and communication.

The Industrial Revolution also prompted reflections on environmental impact, albeit indirectly. The widespread use of coal as an energy source heralded the beginnings of heightened air pollution, a byproduct that would have lasting effects on health and the natural landscape. It was a sign of things to come, forecasting a future where industrial progress would often clash with environmental sustainability.

Yet, through the complex interplay of these transformations, the Industrial Revolution undeniably laid the groundwork for the modern world. It was a time of stark contrasts—progress intertwined with hardship, innovation paired with exploitation. The era sparked the beginning of ongoing conversations about the balance between technological advancement and societal well-being, dialogues that continue to shape our world today.

Innovations of the Industrial Era

The Industrial Revolution marked a seismic shift in the way societies functioned, driven by groundbreaking innovations across various sectors. This era saw the emergence of profound technological advancements that fundamentally altered production methods, transportation, and communication. At the heart of these innovations was the steam engine, which played a pivotal role in powering factories and transforming industries. Initially harnessed for pumping water out of mines, the steam engine's reach soon expanded beyond its humble beginnings.

One major breakthrough was James Watt's enhancement of the steam engine. Watt's modifications included a separate condenser, which significantly improved efficiency and reduced fuel consumption. This engine was more practical and versatile, leading to widespread adoption in textile mills and other manufacturing sectors. With it, the era's motto could have been "efficiency." Factories no longed relied solely on human or animal power; instead, they thrived on mechanical prowess and relentless energy.

Textile manufacturing, indeed, was among the first to experience this transformation. Machines such as the spinning jenny, power loom, and the cotton gin revolutionized the production of fabric and cloth. The spinning jenny allowed a single worker to spin multiple spools of thread at once, dramatically increasing productivity. Meanwhile, the power loom took weaving out of homes and into the factory, paving the way for mass production. These innovations turned Britain into a textile powerhouse and set the stage for the modern garment industry.

Transportation, too, was revolutionized during this time through the development of railways and steamships. The advent of the steam locomotive, exemplified by George Stephenson's Rocket, shrank distances and broke down geographical barriers. Railroads facilitated the rapid movement of goods and people, which in turn stimulated economic growth and urbanization. Cities blossomed around railway hubs, as population centers shifted and expanded along these veins of steel.

Steamships also transformed sea travel. By replacing sail power, these formidable vessels not only increased the speed and reliability of ocean travel but also established new trading routes and lowered the costs of moving goods worldwide. The famous transatlantic steamships were a testament to human ingenuity, connecting continents with a reliability never seen before. The world was becoming smaller and more interconnected.

Communication technology experienced its own revolution, bridging distances with unprecedented speed. Samuel Morse's invention of the telegraph and the Morse code system streamlined communication across vast distances, making it possible to send messages that once took days or weeks in mere minutes. The telegraph knit towns and cities into a web of instant information exchange, fostering new opportunities in trade and coordination.

Yet, the Industrial Revolution wasn't just about mechanical and industrial innovation. In agriculture, the era saw the introduction of new machinery like the seed drill, reaper, and threshing machine. These innovations increased yields and efficiency, which supported growing urban populations and changed how farming was conducted. John Deere's steel plow, for example, made it easier to break the tough prairie sod of the American Midwest, opening new lands for cultivation.

Cultural shifts accompanied these changes in industry and technology. Education became more widespread as societies recognized the need for a more educated workforce to operate complex machinery and manage new industrial processes. The spread of print media, facilitated by advancements in printing technology, meant that information and literacy were no longer exclusive to the wealthy elite.

The changes in workplace dynamics were profound. Factories brought about regimented work environments that contrasted sharply with the agrarian lifestyle that had dominated for centuries. Standardized work hours and factory discipline were new concepts for many people, leading to shifts in how time and labor were perceived. Urbanization followed industrialization, as towns grew into cities fueled by the demand for factory workers. This shift sparked both growth and challenges, such as overcrowding and the rise of tenements.

Despite the breathless pace of innovation and progress, the Industrial Era was not without its critics. The darker side of rapid industrialization included harsh labor conditions, child labor, and massive socio-economic disparities. The seeds of labor movements, strikes, and calls for reform took root during this period, highlighting the need for balance between progress and human values.

The Industrial Revolution paved the way for the modern world, laying down an infrastructure of innovation that future generations would build upon. It was a period characterized by accelerating change, which continues to influence the dynamics of today's societies. This era demonstrated humanity's remarkable capacity to dream, invent, and transform, charting a course toward new possibilities that would make the unimaginable, possible.

Social Repercussions of Industrialization

The Industrial Revolution brought with it a whirlwind of changes that reshaped societies in ways that were as profound as they were revolutionary. As steam engines roared to life and factories mushroomed across landscapes, society experienced shifts that were both exciting and unsettling. Urbanization accelerated at unprecedented rates, drawing people from rural hamlets to burgeoning cities with promises of employment and prosperity. Families found themselves in cramped quarters within soot-smeared cities, marking a departure from the bucolic, agrarian life they once knew.

The migration to urban centers marked a significant transformation in family structures and community dynamics. In rural settings, extended families often lived in close proximity, fostering a strong sense of communal support. This was significantly disrupted as families splintered with individuals moving to cities in search of work. Traditional roles, particularly gender roles, saw a recalibration. Women, who traditionally managed household duties, found themselves working alongside men in factories, weaving fabrics, or assembling parts on a production line. This economic participation, while empowering for some, often resulted in double burdens as women balanced work and family responsibilities.

Child labor became an unfortunate staple of industrial societies, with widespread ramifications on education and health. The demand for cheap labor saw children as young as five years old working long hours in dismal conditions. These children, who might have once roamed fields or attended local schools, were thrust into a world where the clatter of machines replaced the classroom's quietude. While economic necessity pushed families to accept this reality, it spawned movements advocating for educational rights and better working conditions, subsequently leading to significant legislative reforms.

As cities swelled, so too did their challenges. Overcrowding became a critical issue, with infrastructure struggling to keep pace with the influx of inhabitants. Housing shortages led to the rise of slums, where impoverished families lived in squalid conditions without adequate sanitation. The rapid urbanization brought with it public health crises, as diseases like cholera and typhoid fever became rampant. It was a stark reminder of the need for improved public health measures and urban planning, eventually leading to significant advancements in these areas.

The economic disparities that the Industrial Revolution exacerbated were hard to ignore. While industrialists and entrepreneurs amassed wealth, the working class often toiled for meager wages, perpetuating a stark economic divide. The allure of industrial progress became a double-edged sword as it also highlighted the inequalities within society. This undercurrent of discontent fueled movements advocating for workers' rights, giving rise to unions and labor laws that sought to rectify the imbalance in power dynamics between labor and capital.

Another social repercussion of industrialization was the emergence of new social classes. The rise of a wealthy industrial bourgeoisie reshuffled the existing social hierarchy, as this group vied with the traditional landed gentry for social influence. The middle class, composed of educated professionals and small business owners, grew in importance, bridging the gap between the affluent and the impoverished. This transformation in social structure laid the groundwork for modern socioeconomic classes, influencing societal interactions and expectations.

While mechanization improved production efficiency, it also led to the alienation of the worker from their labor—a theme that resonated through the works of philosopher Karl Marx. The factory system, with its rigid hours and repetitive tasks, marked a shift away from artisanal craftsmanship and personal fulfillment through work. Many workers felt like mere cogs within a vast industrial machine, challenging the notion of individual worth and sparking philosophical debates about human purpose in an industrialized world.

Industrialization's influence on arts and literature cannot be underestimated. The gritty reality of industrial life provided a backdrop for realism in literature and art, prompting artists to critique the social impacts of economic progress. The canvas of industrial towns, with their smoke-filled skies and bustling streets, was both muse and commentary on the era's juxtaposition of progress and poverty. Writers such as Charles Dickens and Elizabeth Gaskell painted vivid portraits of life in industrial England, encapsulating the struggles and spirit of the time.

Simultaneously, an increasing environmental consciousness emerged as a direct consequence of industrialization. Factories, while engines of economic growth, emitted pollutants that blackened skies and tainted rivers. The visible despoilment of nature stirred early environmentalist sentiments, leading to movements that advocated for the preservation of natural landscapes and the need for sustainable practices—a theme that gained momentum in subsequent centuries.

The ripple effects of this transformative period extended beyond the immediate confines of industrialized regions, affecting global trading patterns and colonial ambitions. The demand for raw materials and new markets led to the expansion of European imperialism, with industrialized nations vying for control over distant lands. Industrialization thus not only reshaped domestic landscapes but also redefined global interactions, shaping patterns of globalization that continue to resonate today.

In conclusion, the social repercussions of industrialization were as complex as they were profound. These changes laid the foundation for many aspects of modern society, from the urban landscapes we navigate to the social institutions that govern our lives. While the Industrial Revolution was a beacon of progress, it also illuminated the enduring challenges of inequality, labor rights, and environmental stewardship. Despite the passage of time, its echoes remain a significant chapter in the saga of human civilization.

Chapter 8: Colonialism and Its Consequences

Colonialism reshaped entire continents, leaving a lasting impression on both the colonizers and the colonized. At the heart of colonialism was the pursuit of power and resources, often cloaked in a mission of "civilizing" those deemed less advanced. European empires, driven by economic ambitions and a hunger for dominance, stretched their reach to Africa and Asia in ways previously unseen. They established control through a mix of treaties, coercion, and outright conquest.

The impacts of colonialism were profound and multifaceted. Economically, colonies became sources of raw materials and markets for European manufactured goods. This uneven relationship created wealth for the colonizers while stifling the economic development of the colonies. For instance, plantations in Africa and India focused on monoculture, which disrupted local agriculture and made these regions dependent on world market fluctuations. Culturally, colonial powers imposed their values and systems, often at the expense of indigenous traditions. Languages, educational systems, and religions were introduced, fundamentally altering societies.

Politically, colonialism redrew the map of the world. Borders were often arbitrarily determined with little regard for existing ethnic, linguistic, or cultural lines. The legacy of these artificial borders can be seen today in conflicts and tensions across post-colonial states. The imposition of western administrative practices disrupted traditional governance structures, sometimes creating power vacuums filled by opportunistic leaders.

Despite the oppressive nature of colonial regimes, resistance simmered beneath the surface. Nationalist movements began to form, inspired by ideals of self-determination and equality. In India, figures like Mahatma Gandhi championed nonviolent resistance, while African countries saw a rise in educated elites who began questioning colonial rule. This era of decolonization accelerated after World War II, as geopolitical shifts and increasing pressure from independence movements forced colonial powers to rethink their positions.

The path to independence was not without struggle. Some regions witnessed bloody conflicts as the fight for autonomy clashed with entrenched colonial interests. Algeria's battle against French rule and the partition of India, leading to the emergence of India and Pakistan as separate states, are two poignant examples. Decolonization was a complex process that required negotiation and oftentimes involved compromise and conflict.

As former colonies emerged as independent nations, they faced immense challenges. Economics that had been structured to benefit colonial powers struggled to adapt. National identity had to be reconstructed, balancing traditional values with modern aspirations. Yet, in many instances, the legacy of colonial governance left lasting divisions, fueling internal strife and corruption. These young nations embarked on journeys of nation-building with the specter of colonialism casting a long shadow.

The consequences of colonialism still reverberate through the world today. While the era of formal empires may have ended, the systems and structures put in place during this period continue to influence global politics, economics, and cultures. The lessons learned from this era highlight the enduring impact of power imbalances and underscore the importance of understanding the past to navigate the future. Understanding colonialism's complex legacies is crucial in comprehending the modern world's dynamics.

European Empires in Africa and Asia

As the sun set on the medieval period, Europe underwent significant transformations. These changes laid the groundwork for an era of exploration and expansion that would shape the world's continents for centuries. Driven by a mix of ambition, economic interest, and national pride, European powers set their sights on the vast lands of Africa and Asia. The pursuit of new territories was fueled by a thirst for resources, strategic advantage, and the spread of cultural and religious ideologies.

In Africa, the 19th century saw the "Scramble for Africa," where multiple European countries rapidly expanded their influence across the continent. The Berlin Conference of 1884–1885 was pivotal, as European nations carved up Africa with little regard for indigenous cultures or historical boundaries. The conference's goal was to regulate colonization and trade in Africa, leading to artificial national boundaries that would later cause turmoil and conflict.

The British Empire, with its vast reach, established significant footholds in regions such as Egypt and South Africa. The Suez Canal, completed in 1869, was particularly valuable to the British as it provided a direct sea route to India, the jewel in the crown of the empire. In addition, the rich resources in Africa were seen as essential not only for Britain's own industrial needs but also as an opportunity to prevent other European nations from gaining a competitive edge.

Meanwhile, the French established an empire centered in West and North Africa, with territories stretching from Algeria to Senegal. French colonial policy often promoted the assimilation of colonized peoples, theoretically integrating them into French culture. However, in reality, it often resulted in social stratification and the exploitation of local resources and labor. The French administration's emphasis on cultural superiority left lasting imprints on the language, education, and administrative systems in their former colonies.

In contrast, Belgium, under King Leopold II, exerted control over the Congo Basin. Leopold's rule starkly reflected the darker side of colonization, characterized by brutal exploitation and human rights abuses. The extraction of rubber and minerals was prioritized at a horrific human cost, leading to international condemnation and eventually reform of the colonial administration.

While Africa was being divided, European powers also diverted their gaze to the vast reaches of Asia. The British East India Company facilitated the initial British interest in India until direct imperial rule followed the Sepoy Rebellion of 1857. The company's trading posts had evolved into centers of power, showing how trade conduits could transition into political and military strongholds.

The British established an extensive railway network in India, primarily to facilitate resource movement. Although often justified as modernizing influences, such infrastructures served the colonizers' economic interests. India's vast resources of cotton, tea, and spices were exploited for the British market, fueling its industrial complex back home.

Portugal and the Netherlands were early players in Asian trade, focusing heavily on spice-rich regions. The Dutch control of the East Indies (modern-day Indonesia) was lucrative, with spices like nutmeg and cloves driving competition. The Dutch East India Company was among the world's first multinational corporations, wielding tremendous power and influence.

France, in pursuit of showing its own grandeur, consolidated areas in Southeast Asia, leading to the establishment of French Indochina. Through a blend of missionary zeal and economic interest, countries like Vietnam, Laos, and Cambodia came under French control. The cultural exchange was mixed, with French architecture and education systems introduced, yet often met with local resistance.

Colonization wasn't merely a straightforward takeover—it involved complex interaction between colonizers and the colonized. Stories of resistance, negotiation, and adaptation were prevalent. Many colonies adapted European technologies and systems while subtly maintaining cultural practices. This duality bred societies that straddled both worlds, complicating the simplistic narratives of domination.

The consequences of these imperial pursuits in Africa and Asia were profound. Traditional societies were irrevocably changed, often reconstituted around colonial lines. The preference for European legal and educational systems over indigenous ones left lasting marks. Economically, raw resources were extensively mined, enriching the European states at the expense of local economies.

Socially speaking, colonialism introduced significant disruption, breaking down long-established community hierarchies. New social divisions arose, often privileging those who aligned with the powers in charge. The imposed boundaries became sources of ethnic and political conflicts, some of which persist to this day. Beyond economics and politics, the very identities of colonized peoples were reimagined, sometimes erasing centuries of cultural heritage.

However, the resistance against foreign domination also birthed a set of national consciousnesses across these regions, laying early seeds for independence movements. As the 20th century progressed, these colonies would challenge the imperial system, ultimately leading to decolonization and the pursuit of sovereignty.

Reflecting on the European empires' endeavors in Africa and Asia, it is clear their legacy is as much about the unprecedented intermixing of world cultures as it is about conquest and control. This era of history doesn't merely stand as a testament to European ambition but also as a reminder of the resilience and complexity in the human narrative.

Decolonization and the Path to Independence

As colonialism unraveled, the march towards decolonization marked a pivotal chapter in global history. This process, primarily unfolding throughout the 20th century, was as varied as the regions it touched. Different countries experienced it uniquely, influenced by their distinct colonial histories. Yet, the aspiration for self-rule connected these narratives, binding them into a mosaic of liberation and renewed identity.

The struggle for independence could be heard in the impassioned speeches of leaders championing national sovereignty. Figures like India's Mahatma Gandhi, with his philosophy of nonviolent resistance, inspired not only his compatriots but movements worldwide. In Africa, leaders such as Kwame Nkrumah of Ghana and Patrice Lumumba of Congo charted courses that rallied masses with dreams of an autonomous future. Each leader, in their way, navigated the challenges presented by departing colonial powers determined to cling to their diminishing influence.

In many instances, the quest for independence was met with resistance, not just from colonial rulers but also due to internal divisions. This struggle often birthed a political, social, and economic reshuffling as newly independent states sought to define themselves amidst a complex global landscape. The journey wasn't only about the departure of colonial administrators but also the dismantling of entrenched systems and ideologies left behind.

Independence movements were often fueled by cultural renaissance, as colonized peoples sought to reclaim their heritage. The rediscovery of indigenous languages, traditions, and customs became a form of resistance against colonial dominance. This cultural revival wasn't just symbolic but integral to the identity formation of emerging nations. Artists, writers, and musicians became as essential as political leaders in shaping the narrative of new national identities.

Economically, decolonization presented both opportunities and hurdles. The end of colonial rule often left a legacy of skewed economic structures heavily reliant on a few industries or resources. New leaders faced the daunting task of diversifying economies to reduce dependency on former colonial powers. Aligning with global markets provided both hope and challenge as nations sought to find their footing. Some countries, like Malaysia, successfully navigated this transition, while others faced prolonged economic struggles due to factors like corruption or lack of infrastructure.

Politically, the transition to independence wasn't uniform. Some nations transitioned relatively peacefully, establishing new governance structures with little bloodshed. Others fell into cycles of violence and instability, as power vacuums and internal discord erupted. Cold War dynamics further complicated these scenarios, with both Western and Eastern blocs seeking influence over newly independent states, stoking conflicts that occasionally led to prolonged suffering.

For many countries, particularly in Africa, Asia, and the Caribbean, coming to terms with the colonial experience was as much about healing as it was about moving forward. Reconciliation efforts, both among fractured populations and between former colonial masters, marked many post-independence narratives. The importance of this healing process can't be overstated; damaged societies needed time to rebuild trust and forge unified national identities.

Despite the challenges, the period of decolonization also created unprecedented opportunities for innovative governance and social reform. Countries experimented with different political models, seeking what best fit their context. This experimentation was a testament to the resilience and creativity that fueled these fledgling nations' spirits. Nations embraced diverse forms of democracy, socialism, or hybrid systems, often reflective of traditional governance forms reshaped to meet modern needs.

The impact of decolonization stretched beyond immediate political boundaries, influencing global thoughts on sovereignty and human rights. Calls for equality and self-determination reverberated internationally, steering conversations within global institutions like the United Nations. The process laid groundwork for subsequent global movements that would continue to challenge oppressive systems and advocate for marginalized voices worldwide. New geopolitical alliances formed as countries realized the power in unity and cooperation, setting the stage for regional cooperatives like the African Union and ASEAN.

Decolonization, while deeply rooted in its specific historical context, offers a lens through which we can examine current global interactions. The echoes of colonial legacies still manifest in today's societal imbalances and geopolitical tensions. Understanding these historical processes enriches our comprehension of persistent global inequalities and the undercurrents that drive modern international relations.

In reflecting on decolonization, it's essential to remember that it's an ongoing story. While formal colonial rule may have dissipated, neo-colonial influences often persist through economic, cultural, or political means. Efforts to dismantle such influences remain crucial, ensuring the continued evolution towards genuine self-determination and equality. As we view this significant phase in history, it reminds us of the power of resilience, the strength in unity, and the enduring quest for freedom and identity.

Chapter 9:
Wars and Transformations

The human story is one woven with threads of conflict and change, nowhere more evident than in the global hardships and transformations of the 20th century. Clocks ticked forward into an era defined by wars of unmatched scale and the resulting ripple effects that reshaped continents and ideologies. A mere archipelago of alliances initially, the world found itself enmeshed in World War I, a conflict sprawling across borders and oceans.

Technological innovation collided with age-old combat tactics, as mechanized warfare introduced tanks and airplanes. Yet, it wasn't just a battlefield evolution; social structures and political landscapes underwent radical changes, hastening the collapse of empires. Deep in the trenches, the churning mud became a symbol for stagnation and attrition, but above them, empires crumbled, paving the way for new ideologies and nations. The war, often called the "Great War", ironically set the stage for an even greater and more devastating confrontation.

The peace that followed World War I was tenuous, a mere pause rather than a resolution. As nations attempted to rebuild, political ideologies clashed, leaving the world in ideological turmoil. The flames of World War II were ignited as economic despair met with rising totalitarian regimes. This time, the combat alighted on a truly global scale, affecting civilian populations as never before. Battlefields were everywhere, from the beaches of Normandy to the islands of the Pacific.

Nations harnessed new technologies in their quests for dominance, and the war effort became all-encompassing, blurring the lines between military and civilian spheres. This era witnessed the concentration of scientific minds into war efforts, leading to advancements that would later fuel peace and progress. The consequences of this war left a profound impact on the world order. Nations lay in ruins but were ready for transformation.

Out of the ashes of World War II emerged a new world order defined by a bipolar power struggle, yet the immediate task was transformative reconstruction. Nations focused on rebuilding infrastructures and reshaping economies. New global institutions were born to manage international cooperation and forestall future conflicts. The United Nations emerged as a beacon of hope, striving to make peace sustainable, albeit challenged continuously across various geopolitical landscapes. Transformations were underway not just in power structures, but in culture, ideology, and identity.

This period catalyzed innovation and liberation movements, transforming societies and ideologies. Wars and changes, seemingly brutal in their immediate effects, forced societies to adapt and to reconsider old ways of managing power. Economies reimagined themselves, identities were reforged, and the world slowly transitioned into an interconnected system. These transformative forces didn't just reorganize lands; they redefined humanity's approach to conflict, cooperation, and coexistence, setting the stage for the dialectic tensions of the Cold War.

World War I: A Global Upheaval

The world was on the brink of monumental change in the early 20th century. Few events have been as disruptive—or as transformative—as

World War I. This was not just a struggle for territory or power between a few nations; it was a conflict that reshaped the global landscape in ways that resonate even today. While the assassination of Archduke Franz Ferdinand is often cited as the spark, the war's origins were far more intricate, rooted in tangled alliances, nationalist fervor, and a delicate balance of power that tipped disastrously.

Diving into the heart of the conflict, the war's initial stages were marked by rapid movements and hopeful predictions of a swift resolution. But as the initial excitement waned, it became obvious that this war would be long and grueling. The Western Front especially turned into a representation of stalemate and attrition, with its infamous network of trenches stretching across much of Europe. Here, the promise of swift victory was replaced by years of devastating warfare, leaving both land and soldiers scarred almost beyond recognition.

A key aspect of World War I was its introduction of modern warfare technology. From machine guns to tanks, the arsenal of war was forever changed. Artillery barrages and chemical weapons added new horrors and transformed battle tactics. These innovations increased the lethality of war, making it a grim and grinding affair. The resulting devastation extended beyond the battlefield, affecting civilian life in profound ways.

While Europe bore the brunt of the war's fury, its impact was truly global. Colonies were drawn into the conflict, providing both additional troops and resources for their colonial masters. This created a situation where men from Africa, Asia, and other regions found themselves embroiled in a European conflict, often fighting against enemies they'd never even heard of before. This global recruitment laid the groundwork for future calls for independence and sowed seeds of revolution.

The political repercussions of the war were severe. Empires crumbled under its weight—the Austro-Hungarian, Ottoman, Russian, and German empires experienced seismic shifts that led to their eventual disintegration. In Russia, the strain contributed directly to the Bolshevik Revolution, which not only pulled Russia out of the war but also set a new ideological battleground that would fester for much of the 20th century.

At home, nations turned to propaganda to rally support and maintain morale. Government narratives painted the war as a noble cause, urging citizens to do their part through enlistment, rationing, and working in war industries. In many countries, this led to a profound shift in societal roles, particularly for women. The necessity of war had them stepping into roles traditionally held by men, seeding early movements for women's rights and suffrage that would continue to grow after the war's end.

Economically, the war drained national treasures, driving unprecedented borrowing and leading to vast debts that needed to be addressed in its aftermath. The United States, having entered the war later, emerged as an economic powerhouse, setting the stage for its increased influence globally in the years to come. The war's end was marked by the Treaty of Versailles, an agreement that imposed heavy reparations and territorial losses on Germany. Though it officially concluded the war, the treaty sowed dissatisfaction and economic hardship, setting the stage for future conflicts.

The cultural impact was equally significant. Art and literature responded by questioning the values and assumptions that had led to war. Movements like Dadaism reflected the disillusionment and absurdity felt by many, while the "Lost Generation" of writers chronicled the era's desolation. The scars left by the war pervaded every aspect of life and thought, influencing a generation's worldview.

In conclusion, World War I was more than just a global upheaval; it was a catalyst that accelerated change worldwide. It unveiled the precariousness of the existing order and forged new realities. The tremors of this conflict were felt long after the last shots were fired, reshaping societies in ways that remain evident. Understanding World War I allows us to grasp the complex interplay of forces that can erupt into worldwide conflict and emphasizes the importance of learning from history to prevent its repetition.

World War II: A New World Order

Transformations in global power structures have seldom occurred on the scale seen during World War II. The war was not merely a confrontation of military forces but an expansive reshaping of political and social dynamics across continents. It challenged existing paradigms, forging a path toward a new, albeit uneasy, world order.

At the heart of World War II was a clash of ideologies. The rise of fascist regimes in Germany, Italy, and Japan posed a direct threat to the democratic ideals held by the Allied powers, predominantly the United States, the United Kingdom, and the Soviet Union. This ideological struggle wasn't limited to territorial gains but was also about defining the nature of freedom, governance, and human rights.

The war's outbreak in 1939 set the stage for a conflict that would engulf much of the globe. The rapid expansion of Axis powers highlighted weaknesses in the post-World War I settlements, most notably the Treaty of Versailles. While the League of Nations struggled to maintain peace, the dynamic shifts brought about by the aggression of the Axis powers revealed the limitations of existing international diplomacy.

World War II profoundly affected civilian populations. The unprecedented scale of the conflict meant that economies were directed entirely toward war efforts. During this time, technological advancements in warfare, such as radar, jets, and nuclear weapons, progressed with astonishing speed. These innovations had lasting impacts not only on military strategy but also on post-war technological developments.

As the war dragged on, the Allied powers orchestrated numerous operations to counter Axis advancements. Strategic initiatives like D-Day exemplified the Allied commitment to regaining control in Europe. In the Pacific, the United States executed a series of amphibious assaults, eventually leading to critical victories like the Battle of Midway. These efforts turned the tide of war and forged new alliances that would outlast the conflict itself.

The conclusion of World War II saw the collapse of colonial empires and the rise of two superpowers: the United States and the Soviet Union. The bipolar world that emerged set the stage for the Cold War, characterized by ideological conflicts and an arms race which persistently threatened global stability. The United Nations was born out of the desire to prevent future conflicts, embodying a new approach to international cooperation.

War-induced economic shifts were immense. The United States emerged relatively unscathed, becoming a global economic leader. Europe required extensive rebuilding efforts, leading to initiatives like the Marshall Plan, designed to stabilize economies and prevent the spread of communism. Recovery from the war's devastation set the economic groundwork for decades to come.

Societal changes were equally significant. The war catalyzed movements for civil rights and decolonization. The labor force transformation during the war, where women took on roles traditionally held by men, left a legacy of gender role reevaluation. War experiences and atrocities also spurred global discussions on human rights, typified by the Holocaust revelations, leading to the Universal Declaration of Human Rights in 1948.

The diplomatic landscape adjusted in response to new power structures. The fall of Axis powers brought an end to aggressive expansionism but left questions about post-war governance. Newly formed nations sought self-determination, and the shifting political alliances continually redefined continental relationships.

The aftermath of World War II reconfigured global hierarchies, moving away from European dominance toward a more multipolar world. As national borders were redrawn and international policies evolved, the legacy of World War II continued to influence geopolitical strategies well into the future.

Ultimately, World War II wasn't just a test of might but a crucible of change that reshaped societal constructs. It laid the groundwork for contemporary political systems and fostered environments where newly independent nations could assert themselves on the world stage. The war's enduring lessons caution against complacency in maintaining peace while recognizing the transformative potential of cooperative efforts.

Chapter 10: Cold War Dynamics

The Cold War era, a period marked by tension and rivalry, wasn't just a power struggle between the United States and the Soviet Union. It was a global reshaping of political, economic, and social landscapes. This prolonged period of tension saw ideological battles play out not only on a geopolitical stage but also in the very fabric of societies worldwide.

At its core, the Cold War was an ideological clash. On one side, capitalism, championed by the United States, promised individual freedoms and market economies. On the other, communism, as embodied by the Soviet Union, offered an alternative vision of state-controlled economies and collective welfare. These opposing ideologies clashed in countless arenas: in boardrooms, classrooms, and even family living rooms. The world became a chessboard where major powers orchestrated conflicts without ever directly engaging in battle.

Throughout the decades, smaller nations often found themselves pawns or, in some cases, unwilling participants in this grand narrative. The Cold War's shadow loomed large over Asia, Africa, and Latin America, where proxy wars erupted and political dynamics shifted. These regions often became testing grounds for the superpowers' broader ambitions, as both sought to expand their influence. Governments fell, others rose, and the lives of millions were irrevocably altered.

The Cold War also drove technological and scientific innovation. The space race, for instance, was a key arena where both superpowers competed fiercely. The launch of Sputnik and the Apollo moon landings were not just triumphs of human ingenuity; they were declarations of ideological supremacy. Similarly, the arms race, marked by the development of nuclear arsenals, escalated tensions to dizzying heights, affecting global power balances.

Though the Cold War ended with the symbolic fall of the Berlin Wall, its repercussions are still felt today. The ideological battles left an indelible mark on global affairs, influencing political alliances and economic systems. This chapter explores these dynamics, offering insight into how this complex period shaped the world we know now.

Ideological Battles: Capitalism vs. Communism

The Cold War wasn't just a geopolitical tussle; it was a clash of ideologies, each promising a unique vision for humanity's future. Capitalism and communism stood on opposite sides, each a mirror reflecting its own values, aspirations, and economic philosophies. This ideological confrontation became a defining characteristic of the era, fueling tensions that rippled across the globe. The stakes couldn't have been higher, as both systems claimed to offer the ultimate blueprint for freedom, prosperity, and human progress.

On one side, capitalism emphasized the freedom of the individual, where market forces dictated the flow of goods, services, and labor. It was the land of opportunity, where anyone could rise from rags to riches through hard work and innovation. The United States became the poster child of this model, promoting a lifestyle driven by consumerism and technological growth. The promise of capitalism lay in the idea that competition breeds efficiency and wealth, with private ownership being the engine of economic development.

Communism, in stark contrast, preached the virtues of equality and collectivism. It sought to dismantle the class structures that capitalism, at its worst, entrenched. With the Soviet Union as its vanguard, communism championed a world free from exploitation. The state controlled all means of production and sought to distribute resources more equitably among its citizens. Production for use, rather than profit, and the abolition of private property were central to this vision. In theory, this would lead to a classless, stateless society where resources were shared for the benefit of all.

The ideological battleground wasn't confined to theory or state policy—it entrenched itself in every sphere, from textbooks to popular culture. School curriculums across both blocs presented skewed stories, glorifying one's own system while demonizing the other. American media portrayed communists as sinister figures bent on suppressing liberties, while Soviet propaganda painted capitalists as greedy oppressors, eager to maintain the unjust status quo. These narratives influenced perceptions and hardened divides.

In practice, both systems faced inherent contradictions. Capitalism, despite its promises of equality of opportunity, often resulted in stark wealth disparities. Critics pointed to monopolies and corporate power as distortions of its principles. On the other hand, communism, though ideologically aligned with egalitarianism, encountered issues in implementation. The concentration of power in the hands of a few often led to authoritarian regimes, stifling the freedoms it purported to uphold. Ironically, what began as a promise of liberation frequently culminated in repressive state control.

The rivalry was not confined to Europe or the Americas; it went global, casting shadows over Asia, Africa, and Latin America. Each superpower sought to expand its influence by co-opting emerging nations into its ideological fold, offering economic aid, military support, or political alliances. Vietnam, Korea, and Cuba became hotspots where the abstract ideological confrontation turned into tangible conflict. These regions bore the brunt of both superpower interventions, sometimes to devastating effect.

Scientific and technological advancements became another arena of contest. The Space Race exemplified this struggle, with the Soviet Union's launch of Sputnik initiating a fierce competition for domination beyond Earth. This was as much about proving ideological superiority as it was about technological prowess. The decade-long ambition to land on the moon symbolized the American determination to reclaim perceived leadership in human progress.

While the ideological divide dominated international relations, it also inspired profound internal introspection. Within capitalist societies, movements emerged advocating for social welfare, labor rights, and economic oversight, tempering the excesses of unfettered markets. Conversely, some communist states began experimenting with market mechanisms in response to inefficiencies. These shifts indicated that neither ideology was static or monolithic; both systems were evolving through their successes and failures.

The end of the Cold War marked a significant moment in this ideological tug-of-war. As the Soviet Union collapsed and Eastern Europe embraced capitalism and democratic systems, many viewed it as a triumph of the capitalist ideology. However, this didn't signify the end of communism, which persisted and adapted worldwide, most notably in places like China, which crafted a unique blend of communist governance and market-driven economics.

Today, echoes of this historical ideological battle remain relevant. The world witnesses new discussions about the merits and demerits of both systems amidst evolving global challenges. As societies grapple with inequality, climate change, and digital economies, the questions first raised during the Cold War continue to hold significance. Perhaps the ultimate lesson is not the victory of one ideology over the other but the importance of flexibility and adaptation in the face of complex global dynamics.

Cold War's Global Impact

The Cold War wasn't just a period of tension between two superpowers; it was an era that profoundly shaped the global landscape. Stretching from the late 1940s to the early 1990s, this ideological standoff between the United States and the Soviet Union reverberated across every continent, leaving an indelible mark on geopolitics, economics, culture, and beyond. The intertwining threads of fear, ambition, and ideology pulled much of the world into this binary struggle, making their impacts felt far beyond the borders of the U.S. and Soviet territory.

One of the most significant global impacts was the polarization of countries into capitalist and communist blocs. This division wasn't merely a matter of political alignment; it affected economic strategies, military alliances, and even educational systems. Many nations found themselves choosing sides, either willingly or under pressure, leading to the formation of alliances like NATO and the Warsaw Pact. These alliances weren't limited to military cooperation; they dictated economic policies and international relations for decades. Countries often received financial or military aid contingent on their ideological alignment, which in turn shaped their domestic and foreign policies.

Beyond politics and alliances, the Cold War's influence permeated cultures worldwide. Propaganda became a tool of immense importance as each superpower sought to promote its ideology as superior. This led to a proliferation of state-sponsored art, literature, and media, all aiming to win hearts and minds across the globe. Hollywood movies and American pop culture, for instance, became potent symbols of capitalism and freedom, while Soviet films and literature often depicted solidarity, struggle, and unity. This cultural rivalry spurred technological and scientific competitions, most famously manifesting in the Space Race, which captured the world's imagination and drove advancements that have benefited society till today.

While the Cold War avoided direct superpower conflicts, it saw numerous proxy wars around the globe. Regions like Southeast Asia, Latin America, and Africa were arenas where the superpowers backed opposing factions or regimes. The Vietnam War, Korean War, and conflicts in Angola and Afghanistan are just some examples where global Cold War tensions played out with devastating local consequences. These wars often left deep scars, disrupting societies, economies, and political systems for generations. They also highlighted and exacerbated existing tensions and inequalities, contributing to instability that persists in many regions today.

The Cold War also impacted technological advancement and security practices worldwide. The fear of nuclear war, ever-present in public consciousness, spurred an arms race that led to the stockpiling of thousands of nuclear weapons. On the flip side, the necessity for espionage and surveillance pushed technological innovation. Advancements in computing, satellite technology, and spy craft emerged, many of which have evolved into everyday technologies. This period of intense innovation and competition engraved a mindset of strategic risk mitigation that still informs international security policies.

Economically, the Cold War ushered in a variety of outcomes for different regions. For Western Europe and Japan, the Marshall Plan and American economic aid facilitated rapid post-war recovery, transforming these economies into global powerhouses. The Soviet bloc experienced centralized economic control, which brought initial industrial growth but later stagnation. For many developing countries, Cold War politics meant vacillating between aid, interference, and neglect, influencing their paths towards modernization and globalization in complex ways. These impacts were not uniform and often exacerbated local inequalities, leaving legacies that have taken decades to address.

Environmental consciousness also emerged, albeit indirectly, as part of the Cold War legacy. The superpower competition included feats like nuclear testing, which had significant environmental impacts and led to a growing recognition of environmental issues. The process helped galvanize an international environmental movement that began to address issues such as pollution, nuclear disarmament, and sustainability. This reflected a shift in global priorities, illustrating how the Cold War, despite its destructive potential, inadvertently propelled forward a nascent global environmental consciousness.

While this era concluded with the dissolution of the Soviet Union in 1991, the echoes of the Cold War continue to shape international relations and national policies. The structures and alliances created during this time did not dissolve overnight. NATO remains a pivotal military alliance. Formerly communist countries have navigated complex paths toward integrating with the global economy and international community. Meanwhile, countries that used Cold War dynamics to gain leverage or play the superpowers against each other now face the repercussions and challenges of redefining their identities in a post-Cold War world.

In summation, the Cold War's impact on global history is undeniable and vast. Its influence went far beyond a conflict between nations; it sculpted regions, economies, politics, culture, and even technological advancements. The legacy is visible today in divided states, economic policies, cultural dynamics, and the general geopolitical landscape. It serves as a poignant reminder of how ideological rivalry on a grand scale can reverberate through every facet of human society. As we continue to navigate the complexities of modern international relations, understanding this era is crucial for grasping the intricate interplay of past and present on the world stage.

Chapter 11: The Information Age

The Information Age is a period marked by the shift from traditional industry brought by the industrial revolution to an economy based on information technology. It's a time defined by the rapid emergence of digital and cyber technologies that have reshaped societies and transformed the very fabric of global communication. This era began to unfold in the late 20th century and continues to evolve at an unprecedented pace. It has opened doors that were previously unimaginable, allowing instantaneous communication across international borders and democratizing access to information.

This new age saw the birth and swift expansion of the internet, revolutionizing how individuals and organizations interact. Suddenly, entire libraries worth of information became accessible at the click of a button. The internet didn't just change how people access information; it altered how we socialize, shop, work, and entertain ourselves. Social media platforms emerged, shrinking the world into a global village where ideas could be exchanged freely and swiftly, yet with this came challenges of privacy and misinformation.

In the backdrop of this digital evolution, information became a cornerstone of power. Knowledge economies emerged, and companies like Google, Apple, and Microsoft rose to prominence, turning data into one of the most valuable commodities. The Information Age has been marked by incredible achievements in AI, machine learning, and big data analytics, fostering innovations that have led to groundbreaking advancements in fields like medicine, space exploration, and renewable energy.

Yet, the rapid ascendance of digital technologies hasn't come without its societal impacts. The digital divide, cyber security threats, and the loss of personal privacy are some concerns that accompany the benefits of this age. As we navigate these challenges, understanding the influence of the Information Age helps illuminate the paths we tread and the futures we envision. It's a testament to human ingenuity and a powerful reminder of the transformative potential of technology when wielded responsibly.

Digital Revolution: Changing the World

The Digital Revolution, often characterized as the advent of the Information Age, marks a profound era in human history. Unlike any previous epoch, this revolution isn't rooted in land or machinery but in bits and bytes that travel at the speed of light. It's a transformation that has seeped into nearly every facet of life, reshaping economies, societies, and even individual identities.

Initially, the seeds of this revolution were sown in the mid-20th century with the development of electronic computers. However, the real explosion began in the late 20th century when digital technology became accessible to the masses. Suddenly, computing power, once confined to large rooms, found its way onto desks and into pockets across the globe. This democratization of technology set the stage for an unprecedented interconnectedness.

Among the transformative technologies, the internet stands as a cornerstone. It started as a tool for researchers and the military but rapidly expanded into a ubiquitous network that connects billions worldwide. This connectivity has reduced barriers, allowing the instant sharing of ideas, culture, and commerce. Globalization, which had already been in motion, accelerated dramatically, as physical distances seemed to shrink and cultural exchanges became routine.

Moreover, the rise of social media platforms has drastically altered how humans interact and perceive the world. These virtual spaces have become arenas for social discourse, affecting everything from personal relationships to political landscapes. Movements that once took years to build can now gather momentum and incite change in mere days, thanks to the viral nature of digital communication.

Economic structures, too, have been reborn in this digital milieu. The shift from goods-based to information-based economies has been both swift and profound. Intellectual capital has become the keystone of contemporary success, with technology companies now leading the charge as some of the most valuable entities. This shift has sparked new industries, from e-commerce and app development to data analytics and artificial intelligence, propelling countless innovations.

In the workplace, digitization has ushered in a new era of productivity and potential. Automation and information management systems have transformed industries, streamlining processes while increasing efficiency. Yet, these advances also portend challenges, as traditional roles are redefined and certain skill sets become obsolete, demanding constant adaptation and education.

The educational arena is also undergoing a revolution as digital tools expand learning opportunities beyond traditional classrooms. Online courses and mobile applications grant unparalleled access to information, fostering lifelong learning. In some ways, this has leveled the educational field, offering unprecedented opportunities for knowledge acquisition regardless of one's geographic or socio-economic status.

Healthcare has similarly felt the impact, with digital tools enhancing patient care and medical research. Devices that monitor health in real time, combined with telemedicine, have made healthcare more responsive and personalized. This technological integration is paving the way for advancements in disease prevention, diagnosis, and treatment that were once merely aspirational.

Yet, as with any revolution, the digital age isn't without its complexities and contradictions. The very technologies that connect us can also isolate us, as face-to-face interactions sometimes give way to digital interfaces. Privacy concerns have burgeoned as data collection has become pervasive, leading to debates about security and surveillance.

Moreover, the speed of technological advancement often outpaces regulatory frameworks, sparking ethical considerations. Issues of digital equity arise, as not all populations have equal access to technology and its benefits. Bridging this digital divide is a significant challenge that will shape the next phases of this revolution.

The notion of identity itself is evolving under the influence of technology. Digital personas and online anonymity present new opportunities and challenges in understanding self-expression and community. The blending of virtual and real-world experiences prompts a reevaluation of traditional concepts of privacy and personal boundaries.

Furthermore, environmental considerations are increasingly integral to the digital conversation. The sustainability of electronic manufacturing and e-waste management is pressing as the proliferation of devices continues. Here lies a paradox: the digital revolution offers powerful tools for environmental conservation but also introduces new ecological strains.

In essence, the Digital Revolution represents both a continuation and a deviation from past revolutions. Its roots are undeniably intertwined with our collective past, but its branches reach into uncharted territories, challenging historical trajectories and societal norms. As the Information Age continues to evolve, it invites us to continually reassess its implications, demanding thoughtful navigation to harness its full potential for future generations.

Societal Impacts of the Internet

The Internet, a cornerstone of the Information Age, has profoundly reshaped how societies function. It's like a vast digital ocean where information flows at unprecedented speeds, transforming how we connect, communicate, and comprehend the world around us. The effects of this sweeping network have been both liberating and challenging, influencing everything from social interactions to economic landscapes.

In the realm of communication, the Internet has revolutionized the way we interact. Gone are the days when distance was a formidable barrier to connection. Through social media platforms and instant messaging, we can now reach out to friends and family across the globe in mere seconds. This connectivity fosters a sense of global community, enabling cultural exchanges and the sharing of ideas like never before.

However, this digital connectivity isn't without downsides. The brevity and immediacy of online communication can sometimes lead to misunderstandings or over-simplifications of complex issues. Moreover, the anonymity afforded by the web has given rise to phenomena such as cyberbullying and the spread of misinformation. The challenge lies in striking a balance, leveraging the Internet's power for good while mitigating its potential harms.

Economically, the Internet has been a powerful catalyst for change. It's disrupted traditional business models, giving rise to e-commerce and digital entrepreneurship. Startups now have an easier time accessing global markets, leveling the playing field in ways previously unimaginable. Companies like Amazon and Alibaba exemplify this shift, having carved out new commercial landscapes.

Yet, these shifts have brought about significant challenges. The rise of automation and digital platforms has dramatically altered the workforce. Jobs in sectors like retail and manufacturing have been replaced by algorithms and robots. This has provoked debates about the future of work and the necessity of re-skilling programs to prepare employees for a rapidly changing job market.

In terms of education, the Internet has democratized access to knowledge. Online courses and virtual classrooms allow learners from all backgrounds to gain new skills and insights. This democratization offers individuals opportunities for self-improvement and lifelong learning, reshaping educational paradigms.

Nevertheless, the digital divide remains a stark reality. Not everyone has equal access to technology and the Internet. Economic and geographic disparities mean that millions remain disconnected, unable to partake in these digital advancements. Closing this gap is crucial for ensuring equitable access to opportunities in the Information Age.

Social movements have also found a powerful ally in the Internet. Online platforms have become essential tools for organizing, raising awareness, and mobilizing support for causes. Hashtags and viral campaigns can now draw attention to issues that might otherwise remain marginalized in traditional media. Movements like #MeToo and Black Lives Matter owe much of their reach and impact to the connectivity the Internet facilitates.

Conversely, the Internet can also amplify divisive voices and misinformation. Echo chambers and filter bubbles can reinforce existing biases, making it challenging for people with differing viewpoints to engage in constructive dialogue. This paradox highlights the delicate balance between the empowering potentials and perilous pitfalls of the digital world.

Politically, the Internet has transformed not only how campaigns are conducted but also how governments operate. It has enhanced transparency and accountability by enabling citizens to access information and engage in political discourse more actively. Online petitions and social networks allow for greater citizen participation in democratic processes.

On the flip side, the same tools can be used for surveillance and propaganda. Authoritarian regimes have developed sophisticated methods for censoring and controlling online content, using the Internet to curtail rather than expand freedoms. This tension between freedom and control plays out in complex ways worldwide, where the Internet can be both a tool for liberation and a mechanism of repression.

Culturally, the Internet has facilitated the spread and evolution of cultural expressions. Memes, digital art, and streaming services have given rise to new forms of creativity and entertainment, blurring the lines between creators and audiences. This participation has enriched global culture, fostering an environment where diverse perspectives can flourish.

However, this global exposure also challenges cultural preservation. As dominant cultures assert their influence, local traditions and languages face the risk of dilution or disappearance. This underscores the need for intentional preservation efforts to ensure that cultural diversity thrives alongside technological advancement.

Personal privacy has become one of the most pressing issues of the Internet era. With vast amounts of personal data being generated and shared online, concerns about data privacy and security have ballooned. Individuals are grappling with how much of their personal information they're willing to trade for the convenience and functionality that digital services provide.

Regulatory frameworks are continually evolving to address these concerns, yet they often lag behind technological innovations. Companies and governments are tasked with finding ways to protect user data while respecting individual privacy rights. The outcome of these efforts will shape the trust and reliability of the Internet for future generations.

In conclusion, the societal impacts of the Internet have been both transformative and complex. As we navigate this digital landscape, we must consider how best to harness its potentials while addressing its challenges. The interplay between digital connectivity and societal change will continue to shape our world, pushing boundaries and redefining what it means to live in the Information Age. Through careful consideration and deliberate action, we can ensure that the Internet continues to be a force for progress and positive change.

Chapter 12: Lessons from the Past

History has a way of reminding us that the cycles of rise and fall are not just footnotes in textbooks but are the very patterns that shape our world. Through the examination of civilizations like Mesopotamia, Egypt, Rome, and China, we discover a multitude of lessons that offer insights into not only their successes but also their downfalls. These societies, in their grandeur and eventual decline, provide a blueprint for understanding today's geopolitical landscape and the potential futures awaiting us.

Each civilization, despite its unique attributes, follows a surprisingly familiar trajectory. The initial stages often involve a burst of innovation and expansion, as evidenced by the fertile valleys of Mesopotamia or the long-lasting pharaonic dynasties in Egypt. These early successes lay the groundwork for a society's legacy. However, expansion often brings its own set of challenges, from resource depletion to social inequality, both of which can seed the conditions for decline.

Rome, with its unparalleled military prowess and legal systems, is a prime example of a society that commanded the world stage. Yet, internal corruption, economic instability, and external pressures eventually led to its fragmentation. Such patterns of overreach and internal strife can be found echoing in societies across the ages, repeating the age-old narrative that unchecked power and neglect of foundational structures can lead to collapse.

Even amidst these tales of decline, history offers a glimmer of how renewal is possible. The fall of China's Qing Dynasty and the subsequent rise of a modernized state show how rebirth can follow after periods of chaos. Societies have often reemerged with renewed vigor, drawing on lessons from their predecessors to forge a more resilient path forward.

The lessons from these patterns are not just academic. They're blueprints for present and future civilizations. Recognizing the pitfalls of expansion without sustainable foundations, the importance of equitable resource distribution, and the necessity of adaptable governance systems can guide current and upcoming leaders. We stand to learn not only from the successes but more critically, from the mistakes of the past.

Moreover, the blending of various cultural practices has often led to profound advancements, as seen during periods of trade and migration. The cross-pollination of ideas fosters resilience and creativity, reinforcing the idea that open, inclusive societies often enjoy longer periods of stability and prosperity.

As we look to the future, these lessons resonate more clearly than ever. Faced with global challenges such as climate change, economic disparity, and rapid technological shifts, the wisdom gleaned from past civilizations arms us with the knowledge to construct a more sustainable and equitable world. If we choose to heed these historical lessons, we might better navigate the complexities of the present and ensure the stability of societies yet to come.

Patterns of Rise and Fall in Civilizations

The story of civilization is a tapestry woven with the threads of ascension and decline. Throughout history, civilizations have risen to greatness, only to eventually fall, leaving behind a legacy that shapes the world in unforeseeable ways. Understanding these patterns provides valuable lessons about the dynamics of societal change and highlights the factors that contribute to both growth and collapse.

Many historians and scholars have explored the recurring motifs that characterize the evolution of civilizations. A common narrative emerges: societies often ascend through innovation, expansion, and social cohesion. For instance, the Roman Empire's rapid rise was heavily reliant on its military prowess and legal innovations, which facilitated not only territorial expansion but also internal stability. Yet, these very strengths can sometimes become weaknesses. When the expenses of sustaining a vast empire outweigh the benefits, as seen in Rome, decline becomes almost inevitable.

Social cohesion plays a crucial role in the rise of civilizations. At the nascent stages, tightly-knit communities focused on shared goals often thrive. The Han Dynasty of China, celebrated as a golden age, owes much of its success to cultural unity and ideological alignment, fostering economic growth and artistic flourishing. However, as civilizations grow, maintaining this cohesion becomes challenging, leading to internal strife and eventually, fragmentation.

Environmental factors also significantly impact the fate of civilizations. The collapse of the ancient Maya civilization, for instance, is often attributed to prolonged droughts exacerbated by deforestation, leading to severe agricultural setbacks. This scenario paints a vivid picture of how natural events and resource mismanagement can spell disaster for even the most advanced societies.

The interplay between technological advancement and societal structure is another crucial element in this narrative. The Industrial Revolution showcases a period where technological leaps transformed economies and social strata, driving rapid urbanization and new social challenges. While technological innovation can propel civilizations to new heights, as in the case of the digital revolution today, it also has the potential to disrupt existing structures and exacerbate inequalities.

Economic factors have traditionally been both the engine and the Achilles' heel of civilizations. Economic prosperity is a powerful force for growth, as evidenced by the mercantile success of European empires during the age of colonial expansion. However, economic mismanagement, like the hyperinflation that plagued the late Roman Empire or the economic stagnation faced by the Qing Dynasty before its fall, can lead to decline.

Political dynamics are perhaps the most visible aspect of rise and fall. Centralized power, effective governance, and adaptive policies have historically ensured stability and progress. Still, over time, bureaucratic inertia and corruption often creep in. The gradual erosion of political integrity can lead to revolts or even revolutions, as seen in the sweeping changes during the Enlightenment and subsequent revolutions.

Moreover, external pressures from rising civilizations often serve as a catalyst for change. The Mongol invasions reshaped vast regions of Asia and Europe, simultaneously contributing to the decline of existing powers and the rise of new ones. This cycle of conquest and adaptation illustrates how the geopolitical landscape influences the trajectories of civilizations.

Cultural resilience can sometimes act as a buffer against decline. Egyptian civilization, despite numerous invasions and regime changes, maintained its cultural identity through millennia, showcasing the enduring power of culture as a stabilizing force. In contrast, civilizations that fail to adapt culturally to changing circumstances often face existential threats. The Minoan civilization, for example, which relied heavily on a single economic model, couldn't adapt to natural disasters and external pressures, leading to its eventual fall.

What lessons, then, can we draw from these patterns? Recognizing early warning signs of declining stability is key. Environmental sustainability, economic diversification, inclusive social policies, and flexible governance are essential strategies for ensuring longevity. As we face contemporary challenges, from climate change to political polarization, past patterns offer a lens through which to anticipate potential future scenarios.

Studying the trajectory of past civilizations not only satisfies our curiosity about humanity's collective past but also equips us with insights into fostering a more stable and sustainable future. By understanding how civilizations rise and why they fall, we can attempt to carve paths less traveled by the pitfalls of history, potentially crafting a future where stability and prosperity are more widespread and enduring.

Insights for Future Societal Stability

As we journey through the tales of past civilizations, a striking realization emerges: the patterns of rise and fall serve as a guiding compass for future societal stability. Understanding these patterns illuminates the intricate web of factors that underpin societal resilience or lead to decline. So what clues can we extract from history's tapestry to ensure a future of stability and growth?

First, let's consider the role of innovation. Remember how Mesopotamia thrived as the cradle of innovation? This wasn't just luck; it was a bustling hub of creativity and progress. Societies that embrace innovation, as Mesopotamia did, often find themselves better equipped to handle challenges. In today's world, where technology and globalization are reshaping everything from economics to education, nurturing a culture of innovation can be a vital pillar for societal stability. The rapid evolution of digital technologies serves as a modern testament to this age-old lesson. Encouraging open-mindedness and a willingness to adapt can foster environments where innovation thrives. Countries and communities that understand this are those that tend to lead rather than follow.

Yet, with innovation comes another necessity: governance that can manage progress effectively. Ancient Romans might've had their issues, but their legal and governance systems were pivotal in maintaining societal order for centuries. Today, strong governance remains imperative. It can ensure equitable resource distribution, safeguard against corruption, and create frameworks for dispute resolution. These elements maintain societal trust, a fundamental component for any stable society. Without trust, even the most advanced societies can find themselves spiraling into chaos and discord.

Societies also pivot around cultural cohesion and shared values. History shows us numerous instances where cultural discord led to fragmentation and turmoil. The fall of Rome, to some extent, was precipitated by internal disagreements and identity crises. Fast forward to our diverse and interconnected global society, and you'll see the stakes are even higher. Promoting inclusive narratives and recognizing the power of shared identities can fortify societal fabrics. When individuals feel that their cultural histories and identities are valued, there's a greater sense of belonging and willingness to work towards common goals.

Learning from history also involves acknowledging the mechanisms that have led to societal downfall. Environmental degradation, for instance, played a role in the decline of past civilizations, from the deforestation of Easter Island to the over-irrigation in Mesopotamia. Today, as we face urgent environmental challenges, sustainable practices are more crucial than ever. Awareness and proactive strategies in addressing resource management can prevent the societal instability that arises from scarcity and degradation.

On the heels of environmental issues is the pivotal role of education. The spread of Enlightenment ideals was successful largely due to a focus on education and intellectual exchanges. Now, as we navigate complex global challenges, education remains a beacon of hope. Equipping individuals with the knowledge and critical thinking skills necessary to adapt and address these challenges can foster a culture of problem-solvers. By investing in education, societies can ensure a knowledgeable populace capable of making informed decisions.

Conflict and cooperation have always existed as dual forces shaping civilizations. The medieval feudal system, with its rigid hierarchies, may seem archaic, yet it offers a lesson in the dynamics of power and responsibility. Balancing competition with collaboration can drive progress, as cooperation amplifies strengths while reducing weaknesses. Encouraging international cooperation, be it through trade, cultural exchange, or diplomatic alliances, can help build robust systems capable of withstanding internal and external pressures.

Finally, a glance at history underscores the importance of adaptability. Consider China's historical resilience through its complex dynastic cycles. The ability to adapt to changing economic, social, and climatic conditions has often been the difference between societies that flourish and those that falter. Embracing change and fostering an adaptive mindset can be crucial to enduring stability. Societies that resist change are often those caught off guard by inevitable shifts, whereas adaptive societies leverage change as an opportunity rather than a threat.

In essence, the lessons from history serve not just as a recount of past events, but as blueprints for a stable future. The need for innovation, effective governance, cultural cohesion, environmental awareness, education, collaboration, and adaptability are timeless principles that societies must embrace. By integrating these insights, we can hope to build a foundation of stability for future generations, ensuring that the narratives of peace, progress, and prosperity endure through the ages.

Conclusion

As we reach the conclusion of our exploration into the intricate tapestry of human history, it's crucial to reflect on the myriad stories, events, and innovations that have shaped societies across the globe. This journey began at the dawn of civilization with Ancient Mesopotamia, a cradle of innovation, and wound its way through the myriad epochs that have defined human progress. Each stage has left its indelible mark on the fabric of the world, influencing not only the immediate generations but setting the stage for the eras that followed.

History often feels like a procession of empires rising and falling, each leaving behind a legacy that's both a foundation and a lesson. The echoes of Egypt, with its divine order and architectural marvels, resonate through millennia, illustrating the power and reach of human ambition and ingenuity. Likewise, Rome's military prowess and its lasting contributions to law and governance offer timeless insights into the endurance of ideas and institutions.

Throughout this book, we've seen how civilizations like China's dynasties have woven their own distinct threads into the historical narrative. The blend of innovation during the Han Dynasty and the tumultuous transitions leading to modern China present a dynamic story of continuity and change. Similarly, the feudal structures of Medieval Europe laid early frameworks for societal shifts that would eventually propel the continent into periods of significant transformation and renewal.

The Enlightenment heralded an age of reason and reflection, stimulating revolutions that forever altered the political landscapes of nations—the American experience being a prime example. This spirit of change foreshadowed the Industrial Revolution, where technological and socio-economic transformations set humanity on a new path, reshaping how societies function and interact.

But not all transformations have been for the better. The era of colonialism complicated global interactions, with lasting ramifications that are still felt in contemporary society. While the push for independence and self-determination in colonized regions marked significant progress, they were often marred by strife and struggle. These shifts provide a profound understanding of geopolitical dynamics and the complex interplay of power and resistance.

The 20th century brought unparalleled challenges and transformations, with two World Wars and the contentious Cold War period reshaping nations and ideologies. These global upheavals underscored the delicate balance of power and the potential for both constructive collaboration and devastating conflict. The ideological battles between capitalism and communism during the Cold War period were particularly emblematic of the ongoing struggle to find socio-political equilibrium.

Transitioning into the Information Age, humanity has once again entered a phase of rapid evolution. The Digital Revolution has redefined connections, economies, and social interactions, demonstrating both the potential for incredible advancement and the challenges of ethical governance in a digital landscape. The societal impacts of the internet continue to unfold, constantly redefining community and identity on a global scale.

Through these detailed examinations, what emerges is a pattern that history not only repeats but also evolves. Civilizations rise, fall, and transform, often leaving behind a legacy of lessons learned and sometimes unlearned. The resilience and adaptability of human societies underscore a pivotal theme: no matter how daunting the challenges, the quest for innovation and betterment persists.

As history enthusiasts and curious minds have probably gathered, understanding the past involves more than simply knowing dates and events. It's about piecing together the dynamic interactions between cultures, technologies, and ideologies, appreciating their roles in shaping the present and forecasting the future. This book aims to stoke that curiosity and foster a deeper awareness of the complex narrative that is human history.

While we have explored the patterns of rise and fall among civilizations, looking ahead, it is crucial to apply these insights to foster societal stability and progress. The lessons learned from past civilizations highlight the importance of adaptability, innovation, and a cohesive societal purpose in navigating the challenges of the future. The journey of understanding history is never truly complete. It's a continuous process of discovery, offering new perspectives and a deeper appreciation for the interconnectedness of human experience.

In concluding this endeavor, let's embrace the endless curiosity that history demands and continue to delve into the past to discover its lessons for our future. This exploration remains crucial in acknowledging the myriad pathways we've traveled and the potential directions we might yet take. History is not just a backdrop—it's a guide, a teacher, and, at times, a fierce reminder of the human spirit's capability to endure and thrive.

Appendix A: Appendix

In creating this appendix, the aim is to provide readers with valuable additional resources and references that complement and enrich the text of the main chapters. This section includes a collection of maps, timelines, and suggested readings designed to enhance understanding and spark further inquiry into the historical narratives discussed throughout this book.

Maps

- **Ancient Civilizations Map:** This map highlights key regions of development for major ancient civilizations, showing their geographic contexts and the extent of their territories.
- **Trade Routes of the Middle Ages:** Explore the networks that connected different parts of the world through trade in the medieval era, illustrating the flow of goods, ideas, and cultures.
- **Colonial Empires at Their Height:** An overview of the extensive reach of European colonial powers during the 19th century, mapping their territories in Africa, Asia, and the Americas.

Timelines

- **Timeline of Key Events in Ancient History:** A chronological list of significant events from the dawn of civilization through the fall of Rome, helping to visualize the progression of ancient times.

- **Chronology of Revolutions:** Details the series of revolutions following the Enlightenment, including political, social, and industrial changes that shaped modern society.
- **Cold War Milestones:** Focused on the major events and turning points during the Cold War, illustrating the global dynamic between the United States and the Soviet Union.

Suggested Readings

For those eager to delve deeper into specific topics, the following works are recommended:

- *The Epic of Gilgamesh* - A closer look at one of the earliest literary works from Mesopotamia, offering insight into ancient beliefs and societal norms.
- *Egyptian Art and Architecture: The Legacy of the Pharaohs* - This book provides a comprehensive overview of ancient Egyptian achievements in visual and structural arts.
- *Guns, Germs, and Steel by Jared Diamond* - An exploration of the factors that have influenced the fates of human societies throughout history.
- *The Cold War: A New History by John Lewis Gaddis* - A detailed narrative examining the complexities and lasting impact of this pivotal period in recent history.

This appendix serves as a gateway to further exploration and understanding, encouraging readers to build upon the knowledge gained from the main chapters and to engage with history's vast and intricate tapestry.

www.ingramcontent.com/pod-product-compliance
Lightning Source LLC
LaVergne TN
LVHW090328210926
848480LV00004B/1334